Clay County Public
Library
116 Guffey Street
Celina, TN 38551
(931) 243-3442

FALLING WATER REGIONAL LIBRARY

CLY*

D1061364

CRITICAL PERSPECTIVES ON VACCINATIONS

ANALYZING THE ISSUES

CRITICAL PERSPECTIVES ON VACCINATIONS

Edited by Paula Johanson

Enslow Publishing
101 W. 23rd Street
Suite 240
New York, NY 10011
USA
enslow.com

For those we lost to the Spanish flu epidemic

"The mother's battle for her child with sickness, with poverty, with war, with all the forces of exploitation and callousness that cheapen human life needs to become a common human battle, waged in love and the passion for survival."
—Adrienne Rich

Published in 2017 by Enslow Publishing, LLC
101 W. 23rd Street, Suite 240, New York, NY 10011

Copyright © 2017 by Enslow Publishing, LLC

All rights reserved.

No part of this book may be reproduced by any means without the written permission of the publisher.

Cataloging-in-Publication Data

Names: Johanson, Paula, editor.
Title: Critical perspectives on vaccinations / edited by Paula Johanson.
Description: New York : Enslow Publishing, 2017 | Series: Analyzing the issues | Includes bibliographical references and index.
Identifiers: ISBN 9780766081390 (library bound)
Subjects: LCSH: Vaccination—Juvenile literature. | Vaccination—Public opinion—Juvenile literature.
Classification: LCC RA638.J64 2017 | DDC 614.4'7—dc23

Printed in the United States of America

To Our Readers: We have done our best to make sure all website addresses in this book were active and appropriate when we went to press. However, the author and the publisher have no control over and assume no liability for the material available on those websites or on any websites they may link to. Any comments or suggestions can be sent by e-mail to customerservice@enslow.com.

Excerpts and articles have been reproduced with the permission of the copyright holders.

Photo Credits: Cover, funnyangel/Shutterstock.com (syringe), Thaiview/Shutterstock.com (background, pp. 6–7 background), gbreezy/Shutterstock.com (magnifying glass on spine); p. 6 Ghornstern/Shutterstock.com (header design element, chapter start background throughout book.

CONTENTS

INTRODUCTION

The first vaccination was invented by Edward Jenner in 1796, to make people immune to the deadly disease smallpox. By the 1960s, vaccine research had produced several vaccines for immunity against other diseases as well—tuberculosis, polio, tetanus, and more. In the twenty-first century, babies born in North America and Europe are routinely immunized against many diseases that used to be considered "childhood diseases" because almost everyone used to catch them in childhood. Similar vaccination programs can be found around the world in countries that can afford them, with help from the United Nations. Many children used to die from these diseases, and adults, too, if they had never been exposed as children. Travelers can often be exposed to diseases for which they have no immunity, which is why it's important for people traveling overseas to be vaccinated against diseases found at their destinations.

Research into the science of vaccines is ongoing. Scientists are studying new vaccines and are continuing to search for any possible long-term effects decades after vaccination. Their research papers are published in peer-reviewed science journals; colleagues working in laboratories around the world check their lab results and consider their conclusions. But since the majority of people who need vaccination are not medical experts, most people know little of this ongoing research process.

"Since the introduction of vaccination, myths and misconceptions regarding vaccination have been present," notes the European Centre for Disease Prevention and Control (ECDC). "Scientific research in psychology has shown that addressing these misconceptions is difficult: mere reading about a myth, even about a myth's refutation, can strengthen the myth, rather than weaken its influence. Likewise, an explicit and strong negation of a risk can paradoxically increase rather than decrease the perception of risk."

As the ECDC points out, people do not always react rationally to scientific data. Perhaps this is one reason why vaccination has become such a controversial issue in past years.

This book collects articles discussing some of the perspectives people have on vaccinations. Nearly all doctors and medical associations support vaccination, and over 90 percent of citizens get most or all of their recommended childhood vaccinations. But there are a few people and a very few doctors who either do not support the idea of vaccination or do not think vaccinations should be required by law. There are also opportunists and frauds taking advantage of people's fear.

It is hard to write anything about health care that does not make someone upset or uncomfortable.

It's alright to be uncomfortable when thinking about vaccinations. Getting a hypodermic needle in the arm or leg is nobody's idea of fun. Thinking about diseases is upsetting, especially for anyone who has survived one of the many illnesses that people can now be immunized against. Many of these people become angry at the choice of those who decide not to vaccinate themselves or their children, thus putting other community members at risk.

Some of the articles reprinted in this book appeared first in electronic formats with links to detailed footnotes or websites that are mentioned in their texts. All the publications where these articles originally appeared are listed in the bibliography, and readers can find in those original publications all of those details. We encourage you to seek out scientifically supported research, in addition to different perspectives, when making up your own mind about the usefulness and safety of vaccinations.

CHAPTER 1

WHAT THE RESEARCHERS SAY

Research into vaccines is a matter of public record. Anyone can look in journals like *Frontiers in Neurology* to read articles such as "Biopersistence and Brain Translocation of Aluminum Adjuvants of Vaccines." But it takes a lot of practice reading medical jargon to understand that this article's authors studied whether aluminum additives in a few vaccines might be one part of the cause, decades later, of tiny brain changes for a few people with a rare tissue type. Scientists who write in plain language anyone can read, like the famous astronomer Carl Sagan, are rare.

Most vaccine experts are quoted by journalists who write for newspapers, public radio, and popular science websites. A newspaper article called "Traveling Overseas?" will be easier to understand than the journal article it quotes, "Socio-Psychological Factors Driving Adult Vaccination: A

Qualitative Study." Knowing something about statistics might help a reader to understand "A Computational Approach to Characterizing the Impact of Social Influence on Individuals' Vaccination Decision Making." Readers who are not medical experts may try reading just the abstract or summary of an article, as a beginning, to introduce themselves to its content.

"UNDERSTANDING HOW VACCINES WORK," BY THE CENTERS FOR DISEASE CONTROL (CDC), FEBRUARY 2013

Diseases that vaccines prevent can be dangerous, or even deadly. Vaccines greatly reduce the risk of infection by working with the body's natural defenses to safely develop immunity to disease. This fact sheet explains how the body fights infection and how vaccines work to protect people by producing immunity.

THE IMMUNE SYSTEM – THE BODY'S DEFENSE AGAINST INFECTION

To understand how vaccines work, it is helpful to first look at how the body fights illness. When germs, such as bacteria or viruses, invade the body, they attack and multiply. This invasion is called an infection, and the infection is what causes illness. The immune system uses several tools to fight infection. Blood contains red blood cells, for carrying oxygen to tissues and organs, and white or immune cells, for fighting infection. These white cells consist primarily of B-lymphocytes, T-lymphocytes, and macrophages.

- **Macrophages** are white blood cells that swallow up and digest germs, plus dead or dying cells. The macrophages leave behind parts of the invading germs called antigens. The body identifies antigens as dangerous and stimulates the body to attack them.
- **Antibodies** attack the antigens left behind by the macrophages. Antibodies are produced by defensive white blood cells called B-lymphocytes.
- **T-lymphocytes** are another type of defensive white blood cell. They attack cells in the body that have already been infected.

The first time the body encounters a germ, it can take several days to make and use all the germ-fighting tools needed to get over the infection. After the infection, the immune system remembers what it learned about how to protect the body from that disease. The body keeps a few T-lymphocytes, called memory cells, that go into action quickly if the body encounters the same germ again. When the familiar antigens are detected, B-lymphocytes produce antibodies to attack them.

HOW VACCINES WORK

Vaccines help develop immunity by imitating an infection. This type of infection, however, does not cause illness, but it does cause the immune system to produce T-lymphocytes and antibodies. Sometimes, after getting a vaccine, the imitation infection can cause minor symptoms, such as fever. Such minor symptoms are normal and should be expected as the body builds immunity.

Once the imitation infection goes away, the body is left with a supply of "memory" T-lymphocytes, as well as B-lymphocytes that will remember how to fight that disease in the future. However, it typically takes a few weeks for the body to produce T-lymphocytes and B-lymphocytes after vaccination. Therefore, it is possible that a person who was infected with a disease just before or just after vaccination could develop symptoms and get a disease, because the vaccine has not had enough time to provide protection.

TYPES OF VACCINES

Scientists take many approaches to designing vaccines. These approaches are based on information about the germs (viruses or bacteria) the vaccine will prevent, such as how it infects cells and how the immune system responds to it. Practical considerations, such as regions of the world where the vaccine would be used, are also important because the strain of a virus and environmental conditions, such as temperature and risk of exposure, may be different in various parts of the world. The vaccine delivery options available may also differ geographically. Today there are five main types of vaccines that infants and young children commonly receive:

- ***Live, attenuated vaccines*** fight viruses. These vaccines contain a version of the living virus that has been weakened so that it does not cause serious disease in people with healthy immune systems. Because live, attenuated vaccines are the closest thing to a natural infection, they are good teachers for the immune system. Examples of live, attenuated vaccines include measles, mumps, and rubella vaccine (MMR) and varicella (chickenpox) vaccine. Even though these vaccines are very effective, not everyone can receive them. Children with weakened immune systems—for example, those who are undergoing chemotherapy—cannot get live vaccines.

- ***Inactivated vaccines*** also fight viruses. These vaccines are made by inactivating, or killing, the virus during the process of making the vaccine. The inactivated polio vaccine is an example of this type of vaccine. Inactivated vaccines produce immune responses in different ways than live, attenuated vaccines. Often, multiple doses are necessary to build up and/or maintain immunity.
- ***Toxoid vaccines*** prevent diseases caused by bacteria that produce toxins (poisons) in the body. In the process of making these vaccines, the toxins are weakened so they cannot cause illness. Weakened toxins are called toxoid. When the immune system receives a vaccine containing a toxoid, it learns how to fight off the natural toxin. The DTaP vaccine contains diphtheria and tetanus toxoids.
- ***Subunit vaccines*** include only part of the virus or bacteria, or subunits, instead of the entire germ. Because these vaccines contain only the essential antigens and not all the other molecules that make up the germ, side effects are less common. The pertussis (whooping cough) component of the DTaP vaccine is an example of a subunit vaccine.
- ***Conjugate vaccines*** fight a different type of bacteria. These bacteria have antigens with an outer coating of sugar-like substances called polysaccharides. This type of coating disguises the antigen, making it hard for a young child's immature immune system to recog-

nize it and respond to it. Conjugate vaccines are effective for these types of bacteria because they connect (or conjugate) the polysaccharides to antigens that the immune system responds to very well. This linkage helps the immature immune system react to the coating and develop an immune response. An example of this type of vaccine is the *Haemophilus influenzae* type B (Hib) vaccine.

VACCINES REQUIRE MORE THAN ONE DOSE

There are four reasons that babies—and even teens or adults for that matter—who receive a vaccine for the first time may need more than one dose:

- For some vaccines (primarily inactivated vaccines), the first dose does not provide as much immunity as possible. So, more than one dose is needed to build more complete immunity. The vaccine that protects against the bacteria Hib, which causes meningitis, is a good example.
- In other cases, such as the DTaP vaccine, which protects against diphtheria, tetanus, and pertussis, the initial series of four shots that children receive as part of their infant immunization helps them build immunity. After a while, however, that immunity begins to wear off. At that point, a "booster" dose is needed to bring immunity levels back up. This booster dose is needed at 4 years through 6 years old for DTaP. Another booster against these diseases is needed at 11 years or 12 years of age. This booster for older children—and teens and adults, too—is called Tdap.
- For some vaccines (primarily live vaccines), studies

have shown that more than one dose is needed for everyone to develop the best immune response. For example, after one dose of the MMR vaccine, some people may not develop enough antibodies to fight off infection. The second dose helps make sure that almost everyone is protected.

- Finally, in the case of the flu vaccine, adults and children (older than 6 months) need to get a dose every year. Children 6 months through 8 years old who have never gotten the flu vaccine in the past or have only gotten one dose in past years need two doses the first year they are vaccinated against flu for best protection. Then, annual flu shots are needed because the disease-causing viruses may be different from year to year. Every year, the flu vaccine is designed to prevent the specific viruses that experts predict will be circulating.

THE BOTTOM LINE

Some people believe that naturally acquired immunity—from having the disease itself—is more effective than the immunity provided by vaccines. However, natural infections can cause severe complications and be deadly. This is true even for diseases that most people consider mild, like chickenpox. It is impossible to predict who will get serious infections that may lead to hospitalization.

Vaccines, like any medication, can cause side effects. The most common side effects are mild. However, many vaccine-preventable disease symptoms can be serious, or even deadly. Although many of these diseases are rare in this country, they do circulate around the world and can be brought into the U.S., putting unvaccinated children at risk. Even with advances in health care, the diseases that vaccines prevent can still be very serious—and vaccination is the best way to prevent them.

1. According to this article, how do our bodies fight germs that cause disease?
2. Why is getting vaccinated better than becoming ill with most of these diseases?

"HOW TO READ AND UNDERSTAND A SCIENTIFIC PAPER: A GUIDE FOR NON-SCIENTISTS," BY JENNIFER RAFF, FROM *VIOLENT METAPHORS*, AUGUST 25, 2013

Last week's post (The truth about vaccinations: Your physician knows more than the University of Google) sparked a very lively discussion, with comments from several people trying to persuade me (and the other readers) that *their* paper disproved everything that I'd been saying. While I encourage you to go read the comments and contribute your own, here I want to focus on the much larger issue that this debate raised: what constitutes scientific authority?

It's not just a fun academic problem. Getting the science wrong has very real consequences. For example, when a community doesn't vaccinate children because they're afraid of "toxins" and think that prayer (or diet, exercise, and "clean living") is enough to prevent infection, outbreaks happen.

> "Be skeptical. But when you get proof, accept proof." –Michael Specter

What constitutes enough proof? Obviously everyone has a different answer to that question. But to form a truly educated opinion on a scientific subject, you need to become familiar with current research in that field. And to do that, you have to read the "primary research literature" (often just called "the literature"). You might have tried to read scientific papers before and been frustrated by the dense, stilted writing and the unfamiliar jargon. I remember feeling this way! Reading and understanding research papers is a skill which every single doctor and scientist has had to learn during graduate school. You can learn it too, but like any skill it takes patience and practice.

I want to help people become more scientifically literate, so I wrote this guide for how a layperson can approach reading and understanding a scientific research paper. It's appropriate for someone who has no background whatsoever in science or medicine, and based on the assumption that he or she is doing this for the purpose of getting a basic understanding of a paper and deciding whether or not it's a reputable study.

The type of scientific paper I'm discussing here is referred to as a **primary research article**. It's a peer-reviewed report of new research on a specific question (or questions). Another useful type of publication is a **review article**. Review articles are also peer-reviewed, and don't present new information, but summarize multiple primary research articles, to give a sense of the consensus, debates, and unanswered questions within a field. (I'm not going to say much more about them here, but be cautious about which review articles you read. Remember that they are only a snapshot of the research at the time they are published. A review article on, say, genome-wide association studies from 2001 is not going to be very informative in 2013. So much research has been done in the intervening years that the field has changed considerably.)

BEFORE YOU BEGIN: SOME GENERAL ADVICE

Reading a scientific paper is a completely different process than reading an article about science in a blog or newspaper. Not only do you read the sections in a different order than they're presented, but you also have to take notes, read it multiple times, and probably go look up other papers for some of the details. Reading a single paper may take you a very long time at first. Be patient with yourself. The process will go much faster as you gain experience.

Most primary research papers will be divided into the following sections: Abstract, Introduction, Methods, Results, and Conclusions/Interpretations/Discussion. The order will depend on which journal it's published in. Some journals have additional files (called Supplementary Online Information), which contain important details of the research, but are published online instead of in the article itself (make sure you don't skip these files).

Before you begin reading, take note of the authors and their institutional affiliations. Some institutions (e.g. University of Texas) are well-respected; others (e.g. the Discovery Institute) may appear to be legitimate research institutions but are actually agenda-driven. *Tip: google "Discovery Institute" to see why you don't want to use it as a scientific authority on evolutionary theory.*

Also take note of the journal in which it's published. Reputable (biomedical) journals will be indexed by Pubmed. **[EDIT: Several people have reminded me that non-biomedical journals won't be on Pubmed, and they're absolutely correct! (Thanks for catching that, I apologize for being sloppy here.) Check out Web of Science for a more complete index of science journals. And please feel free to share other resources in the comments!]** Beware of questionable journals.

As you read, write down **every single word** that you don't understand. You're going to have to look them all up (yes, every one. I know it's a total pain. But you won't understand the paper if you don't understand the vocabulary. Scientific words have extremely precise meanings.).

STEP-BY-STEP INSTRUCTIONS FOR READING A PRIMARY RESEARCH ARTICLE

1. BEGIN BY READING THE INTRODUCTION, NOT THE ABSTRACT.

The abstract is that dense first paragraph at the very beginning of a paper. In fact, that's often the only part of a paper that many non-scientists read when they're trying to build a scientific argument. (This is a terrible practice—don't do it.) When I'm choosing papers to read, I decide what's relevant to my interests based on a combination of the title and abstract. But when I've got a collection of papers assembled for deep reading, I always read the abstract last. I do this because abstracts contain a succinct summary of the entire paper, and I'm concerned about inadvertently becoming biased by the authors' interpretation of the results.

2. IDENTIFY THE BIG QUESTION.

Not "What is this paper about." but "What problem is this entire field trying to solve?"

This helps you focus on why this research is being done. Look closely for evidence of agenda-motivated research.

3. SUMMARIZE THE BACKGROUND IN FIVE SENTENCES OR LESS.

Here are some questions to guide you:

What work has been done before in this field to answer the BIG QUESTION? What are the limitations of that work? What, according to the authors, needs to be done next?

The five sentences part is a little arbitrary, but it forces you to be concise and really think about the context of this research. You need to be able to explain why this research has been done in order to understand it.

4. IDENTIFY THE SPECIFIC QUESTION(S)

What **exactly** are the authors trying to answer with their research? There may be multiple questions, or just one. Write them down. If it's the kind of research that tests one or more null hypotheses, identify it/them.

Not sure what a null hypothesis is? Go read this, then go back to my last post and read one of the papers that I linked to (like this one) and try to identify the null hypotheses in it. Keep in mind that not every paper will test a null hypothesis. [Editor's note: Links in this post are included in the Chapter Notes at the end of this book.]

5. IDENTIFY THE APPROACH

What are the authors going to do to answer the SPECIFIC QUESTION(S)?

6. Now read the methods section. Draw a diagram for each experiment, showing exactly what the authors did.

I mean *literally* draw it. Include as much detail as you need to fully understand the work. As an example, here is what I drew to sort out the methods for a paper I read today (Battaglia et al. 2013: "The first peopling of South America: New evidence from Y-chromosome haplogroup Q"). *[Editor's note: Images are not included in this book, but can be found online with the original article.]* This is much less detail than you'd probably need, because it's a paper in my specialty and I use these methods all the time. But if you were reading this, and didn't happen to know what "process data with reduced-median method using Network" means, you'd need to look that up.

You don't need to understand the methods in enough detail to replicate the experiment—that's something reviewers have to do—but you're not ready to move on to the results until you can explain the basics of the methods to someone else.

7. READ THE RESULTS SECTION. WRITE ONE OR MORE PARAGRAPHS TO SUMMARIZE THE RESULTS FOR EACH EXPERIMENT, EACH FIGURE, AND EACH TABLE. DON'T YET TRY TO DECIDE WHAT THE RESULTS *MEAN*, JUST WRITE DOWN WHAT THEY *ARE*.

You'll find that, particularly in good papers, the majority of the results are summarized in the figures and tables. Pay careful attention to them! You may also need to go to the Supplementary Online Information file to find some of the results.

It is at this point where difficulties can arise if statistical tests are employed in the paper and you don't have enough of a background to understand them. I can't teach you stats in this post, but here, here, and here are some basic resources to help you. I STRONGLY advise you to become familiar with them.

THINGS TO PAY ATTENTION TO IN THE RESULTS SECTION:

- Any time the words "significant" or "non-significant" are used. These have precise statistical meanings. Read more about this here.
- If there are graphs, do they have error bars on them? For certain types of studies, a lack of confidence intervals is a major red flag.
- The sample size. Has the study been conducted on 10, or 10,000 people? (For some research purposes, a sample size of 10 is sufficient, but for most studies larger is better.)

8. DO THE RESULTS ANSWER THE SPECIFIC QUESTION(S)? WHAT DO YOU THINK THEY MEAN?

Don't move on until you have thought about this. It's okay to change your mind in light of the authors' interpretation—in fact you probably will if you're still a beginner at this kind of analysis—but it's a really good habit to start forming your own interpretations before you read those of others.

9. READ THE CONCLUSION/DISCUSSION/INTERPRETATION SECTION.

What do the authors think the results mean? Do you agree with them? Can you come up with any alternative way of interpreting them? Do the authors identify any weaknesses in their own study? Do you see any that the authors missed? (Don't assume they're infallible!) What do they propose to do as a next step? Do you agree with that?

10. NOW, GO BACK TO THE BEGINNING AND READ THE ABSTRACT.

Does it match what the authors said in the paper? Does it fit with your interpretation of the paper?

11. FINAL STEP: *(DON'T NEGLECT DOING THIS)* WHAT DO OTHER RESEARCHERS SAY ABOUT THIS PAPER?

Who are the (acknowledged or self-proclaimed) experts in this particular field? Do they have criticisms of the study that you haven't thought of, or do they generally support it?

Here's a place where I do recommend you use Google! But do it last, so you are better prepared to think critically about what other people say.

(12. This step may be optional for you, depending on why you're reading a particular paper. But for me, it's critical! I go through the "Literature cited" section to see what other papers the authors cited. This allows me to better identify the important papers in a particular field, see if the authors cited my own papers (KIDDING!....mostly), and find sources of useful ideas or techniques.)

1. Why are scientific papers available for people to read who don't have a science degree?
2. What can a student or untrained adult learn from a paper written by a medical scientist for scientists?

"VACCINE STUDY AIMS TO BUILD COMMON GROUND FOR PARENTS, SCIENTIFIC COMMUNITY," BY LAUREN LOFTUS, FROM *CRONKITE NEWS*, OCTOBER 2, 2014

PHOENIX – Parents deciding whether or not to vaccinate their children can be made to feel paranoid by health care providers for voicing any concerns.

To Ken Roland, research associate professor at Arizona State University's Biodesign Institute, scientists should learn how to communicate better to bridge the gap with these concerned parents and build common ground.

"The problem that we have as scientists is we're not really trained to be public speakers," said Roland, who contributed to a recent study aimed at raising vaccine awareness. The institute collaborated with the Centre for the Study of Sciences and the Humanities at the University of Bergen, Norway.

The study examines ways to establish an open dialogue between members of the scientific community and members of the general public about scientific innovations such as new vaccines.

"We (scientists) tend to have a certain way of thinking about the world that's cut-and-dry," Roland said. "That's not necessarily going to resonate with other people."

Specifically, the study highlighted a new breed of vaccines known as Recombinant Attenuated Salmonella Vaccines. Roland explained that the bacteria salmonella is used as a vehicle to deliver proteins that could protect against a variety of bacterial infections like whooping cough.

But because they're using salmonella, Roland said his team is trying to get out ahead of any public misinformation or misconceptions.

"Everybody knows salmonella makes you sick right, so why would you use salmonella?" he said.

But once scientists restructured the salmonella genome to avoid causing disease, Roland said "it turns out salmonella is very good at eliciting immune responses."

Dorothy Dankel, a scientist at the University of Bergen who co-authored the study, said the study takes a "common-sense approach" that moves away from the typical, top-down model of the scientific community. She said there's a misconception among scientists that if people have just the facts, they'll automatically be on their side.

"Seventy percent of our decisions are emotional decisions," Dankel explained. "You have to understand people's values and speak to those values."

That emotion could explain why a growing number of parents are choosing not to vaccinate their children.

According to immunization data reports from the Arizona Department of Health Services, the percentage of children not being vaccinated for personal or religious reasons has steadily increased over the last decade.

In Maricopa County, the personal exemption rate for sixth-graders was 5.2 percent for the 2013–2014 school year, up 1 percentage point from the previous year. For kindergartners, the personal exemption rate increased from 4.3 to 5.1 percent in that same time.

Jessica Rigler, chief for the Bureau of Epidemiology and Disease Control at the department, said certain pockets of individual communities are primarily responsible for the dropping levels of immunized kids. She said it's most common in communities with higher incomes and higher levels of education.

"We like to have our vaccination rates about 95 percent or above for most vaccine preventable diseases, because that's the level of what we'd consider herd immunity," Rigler said.

Herd immunity refers to a level of immunity achieved when enough members of a population are vaccinated against an infectious disease so they can protect others who haven't developed immunity.

State Sen. Debbie McCune Davis, D-Phoenix, executive director of The Arizona Partnership for Immunization, called it a pattern of parents being more choosy about vaccinations when disease is less prevalent.

"Vaccines are really a victim of their own success," she said. "When disease is prevalent, the vaccine is accepted. But after the vaccine produces the result where the disease is no longer visible, then the vaccine becomes the threat."

In order to combat this pattern, McCune Davis said her organization produces educational materials for doctors to give parents a better understanding of how vaccinations work. But the most important thing, she said, is that doctors explain that the primary objective is to keep children healthy.

Stephanie Sergo, a stay-at-home mother of four in San Tan Valley, said that the decision to vaccinate is ultimately up to the parents.

When her youngest was 6 months old, Sergo said she had a gut feeling that she shouldn't get the recommended booster shots because her daughter was experiencing problems breathing.

"If you get vaccines with children when they're sick, it can cause complications. I feel like they don't stress that enough at doctor's offices," she said.

After her daughter recovered, Sergo eventually did get her up-to-date on vaccines.

Sergo said her pediatrician was supportive but that not everyone is so lucky.

"A lot of times you can get doctors who treat you like a bad parent if you don't want to do it," she said. "They look at you like you have another head if you have any concerns."

Sergo said she would welcome a movement from the scientific community to build an "atmosphere of understanding" with parents.

At ASU, Ken Roland said that was the motivation for participating in the study.

"We're part of the same community as other folks, and these vaccines are going to impact us as well as everyone else," he said. "We don't want to put out something that's going to harm anyone ... we don't have any special agenda."

1. In your opinion, why is there a lack of trust between scientists (such as medical researchers of vaccines) and ordinary people?

"EDITORIAL: IMPORTANCE OF TIMELY MONITORING OF SEASONAL INFLUENZA VACCINE EFFECTIVENESS,"BY RICHARD PEBODY AND KÅRE MØLBAK, FROM *EUROSURVEILLANCE*, APRIL 21, 2016

Seasonal influenza vaccination programmes represent one [of] the largest components of national immunisation programmes in many industrialised countries with a wide range of target groups in the population. These programmes target groups at higher risk of severe disease including the elderly, those with underlying clinical risk factors and pregnant women in many European countries. [1] Additionally many countries offer vaccines to healthcare workers and some to healthy children. [1] The rationale for vaccinating the latter is to both directly protect the vaccinated persons themselves by reducing the spread of infection and indirectly protect other groups at higher risk of severe disease whether that is in the local community or the hospital where they work.

Due to changes in the dominant circulating strains each season and the limited length of protection [2] afforded by the current generation of influenza vaccines, countries undertake annual vaccination campaigns. These time-limited programmes are usually conducted in the period just prior to the start of the influenza season to maximise population protection. Annual public health monitoring of the effectiveness of seasonal influenza vaccine has now become well established in North America, Europe and Australasia to complement existing virological surveillance and characterisation of circulating strains. Countries use the test-negative case-control approach through established sentinel primary care swabbing networks or comparable data sources, with many countries undertaking mid-season vaccine effectiveness (VE) estimates. [3] These early-season estimates are important for several reasons. Firstly, together with available virus characterisation data, they provide an early indication of how well the current season's vaccine is (or is not) matched to the circulating strains: this enables public health measures to be refined if necessary e.g. the use of antivirals to further reduce the health impact of influenza. VE measures combined with estimates and projections of number of hospital admissions related to influenza are also important for healthcare service planning and situational awareness. Finally, the information from these mid-season VE estimates is provided to the World Health Organization (WHO) twice-yearly convened influenza vaccine composition meeting by the Global Influenza Vaccine Effectiveness collaboration together with virological characterisation and serological data. [4] This group recommends the content of the seasonal influenza vaccine for the northern and southern hemispheres that vaccine manufacturers need to produce ready for the vaccine campaigns six months later. These estimates are importantly provided independent of the vaccine manufacturers, who are required to submit safety and effectiveness data as part of recently introduced European Medicines Agency requirements. [5]

Two papers in this week's edition of *Eurosurveillance* highlight further the importance of this timely seasonal influenza VE monitoring in optimising seasonal influenza vaccination strategies [6,7] while a third addresses pandemic vaccination strategies in the Nordic countries, 2009 [8]. The more ready availability of epidemiological VE data has provided the WHO committee with further and timelier insights into the match between circulating and vaccine strains and enhances its ability to make the best recommendations possible about the vaccine strain composition for the forthcoming season using epidemiological, virological and serological data. The first paper by Leung et al., a systematic review over almost a decade, reinforces this point, with the article demonstrating the usual reliability of these early-season VE estimates when compared to the final end-of-season estimates. The authors also demonstrate that in the majority of studies, the mid-season VE estimates were within 10% of the final end-of-season estimate, with the vast bulk of the interim estimates provided ahead of the WHO influenza vaccine composition meeting. The paper also highlights the importance of ensuring a standard approach to enhance the comparability between mid- and end-of-season VE, and that protocols need to meet this aim.

The second paper by Kissling et al. from the European I-MOVE network examines the important question of whether there is any evidence of intra-seasonal waning of VE over the period from 2010/11 to 2014/15. They demonstrate evidence of consistent reductions in VE against A(H3N2) to 0% by >three months after vaccination across all seasons examined; with smaller reductions for influenza B and a stable VE against A(H1N1)pdm09 throughout the season. They discuss potential explanations for these observations in particular disentangling intra-seasonal waning of vaccine-derived immunity versus changes in circulating strains which may be antigenically mismatched later in the season. Interestingly the waning findings are mainly restricted to A(H3N2). This subtype is recognised to be challenging as a vaccine target, and which mainly results in health impact in the elderly. From the paper by Leung et al., the overall population impact of this 'waning' of VE can be seen when comparing the mid and end-of-season estimates, reinforcing the findings from Kissling et al. [7] The reductions in VE on the population level are likely to be more apparent when A(H3N2) circulates later in the season, as was the case in 2013/14, when a number of countries reported evidence of reductions in A(H3N2) VE later in the season.

Whatever the explanation for these observations, the findings of intra-seasonal waning raise important questions about what the optimal intervention strategy is. The authors propose undertaking campaigns later in the season. Practically, this would be a challenging policy to implement, particularly in larger temperate countries. With the timing of influenza activity so variable each year and the season usually lasting at least 6 to 8 weeks; campaigns in the northern hemisphere need to be largely completed by end of December before the season starts. As vaccine is only available usually from October onwards and the delivery of the annual campaign requires several weeks of intensive vaccination activity (including two weeks for protection to be acquired), there is little flexibility in timing, without taking real risks of not providing the population protection required before influenza circulation starts. What strategies might be employed otherwise? Even in an optimal scenario with a good match between the circulating influenza strain and the vaccine, and with a timing of the season in favour of the vaccine, the effectiveness is less than other vaccines offered in the childhood vaccination programmes. Although there is a clear need for new and better influenza vaccines, possibly targeting conserved antigens; there is also a need to identify which of the existing available influenza vaccines e.g. adjuvanted and high dose inactivated or quadrivalent versus trivalent, might provide optimal protection in key target groups, particularly the elderly where the impact of A(H3N2) is usually greatest. How these vaccines might be used better should also be considered as highlighted by Kissling et al., VE depends on age, and although the sample size of their study was not big enough to determine if there was waning immunity in smaller age strata, one question might be if waning vaccine-derived immunity against influenza A(H3N2) is less of a problem in the younger age groups. This would be supportive of another intervention strategy, where the primary focus would be preventing the spread of influenza to groups at higher risk of severe disease by vaccinating children. This approach of trying to provide both direct and indirect population protection is currently being introduced in the United Kingdom through a new vaccination programme of healthy children with live attenuated influenza vaccine. As also mentioned by Kissling et al., the current season influenza VE may vary by prior influenza vaccine history, and there is a need to understand this better to ensure optimal intervention strategies are developed. This strategy is also supported in a third paper by Gil Cuesta et al. [8] also published in this issue, that demonstrates lower cumulative rates of influenza A(H1N1)pdm09 infection in the influenza season following the 2009 pandemic in the four of five Nordic countries with higher pandemic vaccine coverage in the wider general population, including children. This indicates that in the assessment of impact of vaccination strategy, it may be important to look at more than one season, possibly taking type of vaccine and age-group targeted into account.

It is also important to note that there are other interventions than vaccines. Public health authorities need to consider how the use of antiviral drugs might be optimised to further reduce morbidity and mortality particularly when influenza seasons are unusually late. Finally, behavioral measures such as hand hygiene, avoiding close contact to sick persons, staying home when sick and cough etiquette are measures that can contribute to prevention of the spread of influenza throughout the influenza season.

1. What are some ways medical researchers evaluate the efficacy of vaccination programs?

"GILBERT DOCTOR'S PUSH FOR VACCINATIONS IS PERSONAL AND PROFESSIONAL," BY MIRANDA LEO, FROM *CRONKITE NEWS*, FEBRUARY 10, 2015

WASHINGTON – Gilbert pediatrician Tim Jacks was in Washington Tuesday to testify on the importance of vaccination, but he told senators that he was there not as a doctor but as a father.

Jacks' two children cannot be vaccinated – one is too young and one is weaked by leukemia – and are now in quarantine to see if they show symptoms of measles after being exposed to a measles-infected patient at a clinic recently.

The best protection for people like his children, Jacks said in testimony to the Senate Health, Education, Labor and Pensions Committee, is for others around them to be vaccinated.

"As immunization rates drop, herd immunity starts to break down. And this herd immunity is the only thing protecting my two young children from being exposed to measles or whatever the next problem is," Jacks testified.

Jacks was part of a panel of doctors speaking before a largely supportive committee on the necessity of vaccines after a measles outbreak in California that has since spread to six other states. The Centers for Disease Control and Prevention reported last week that 114 people had been infected as a result, including seven in Arizona.

Many of the panelists pointed to what they called unfounded fears about the safety of vaccines as the reason for an increase in the number of parents who are choosing not to immunize their kids. That, in turn, has led to the spread of illnesses, like measles, that were thought to be eradicated in the U.S.

That trend has been seen in Arizona, where the number of vaccination exemption due to personal belief has risen from 1.6 percent a decade ago to 3.9 percent in 2012–2013, according to the Arizona Department of Health Services.

"Once the fear is out there it takes a lot to reassure, it takes a long time before that leaves the memory of somebody," Jacks said after his testimony.

Sen. Michael Bennet, D-Colo., said those trying to encourage vaccinations appear to have "been victimized by two things."

"One, a generation that has not experienced these diseases because of vaccines and have lost sight of what they look like," Bennet said at Tuesday's hearing. "And … the unedited content on the Internet that people, I guess more affluent families, are reading."

As a pediatrician, Jacks said he strongly encourages all of his patients to get the regular regimen of vaccinations. Despite the grief it has caused his family, however, he also said he still believes parents should have the ability to make their own choices about vaccinating their children – but he does think it should be harder for parents to opt out.

The problem with allowing people to choose not to be immunized, as Jacks noted, is that such choices affect other people as well.

That was the case for his family. After his daughter's regular visit to a clinic for her leukemia on a Wednesday, the clinic called the following Sunday to say that Jacks, his daughter, his son and his wife had all been exposed to measles due to another patient.

Because of their lack of immunity, Jacks' children had to return to the hospital for an emergency shot of measles anti-bodies. They now must wait to see if the children develop symptoms, which they have not yet.

Since the ordeal began, Jacks' blog postings on the topic have gained a national audience allowing him a larger platform from which to calm parents' fears about vaccines that might cause them to opt out of immunizing their children.

"My hope is that we can prevent some families from going through the same thing that we've gone through these past few weeks," he said. "Prevention is simple. Vaccinate."

1. What is "herd immunity"?
2. Why are some children medically unable to receive vaccines? Why would they then be dependent on herd immunity?

CHAPTER 2

WHAT THE GOVERNMENT AND POLITICIANS SAY

Most Western countries have policies recommending vaccination for all persons. Included in this chapter are articles from government agencies showing typical recommendations for adults and children. However, these governmental policies are relatively recent. "In 1969, New York became the first state to enact a compulsory school vaccination law," author Seth Mnookin notes in *The Panic Virus*. "By the mid-1970s, thirty-nine other states had followed suit. The rapid expansion of vaccination law established freedom from disease as a national priority and not just an individual prerogative." Similar laws passed in many nations around the world around this time.

Since vaccination was first recommended by councils of physicians, doctors and governments have recognized that there are two groups of people exempt from vaccination programs. These exemptions add up to fewer than 5 percent of the population. People who receive a medical exemption have one of several conditions, and most often an immune system problem, which means they should not be vaccinated. A so-called conscientious exemption, meaning moral or religious reasoning against vaccinations, was until recently called for only by people of Anabaptist faiths—these Amish, Hutterites, and Mennonites are also allowed by the government to be conscientious objectors during times of war. Almost all other religions support vaccination programs.

Today, however, some parents in the United States and Canada who aren't Anabaptist are demanding a conscientious exemption for their children. In some states, laws are being passed that restrict conscientious exemption only to adults, and enforcing vaccination for children who attend schools and daycares.

"A PARENT'S GUIDE TO VACCINATION," BY THE GOVERNMENT OF CANADA, FROM HEALTHY LIVING, UPDATED DECEMBER 24, 2015

Vaccination is the best way to protect your child's health.

Parents are responsible for the well-being of their children, including protecting them from illness caused by diseases that are vaccine-preventable. Learn about vaccination and why it is important to your child's health.

Parents agree that feeding and sleeping schedules are important to help keep children healthy. The same goes for childhood vaccinations. Vaccinating your children is the best way to keep them safe from many serious and potentially deadly diseases. You can help protect your children by getting them vaccinated on time and keeping their shots up-to-date.

WHAT IS A *VACCINE?*

Vaccines are made with a tiny amount of dead or weakened germs. They help the immune system learn how to protect itself against disease. Vaccines are a safe and effective way to keep your child from getting very sick from the *real* disease.

Did you know?

Vaccination can also be called immunization, vaccines, shots, or needles. These words mean the same thing.

WHAT IS THE IMMUNE SYSTEM?

The immune system is a special network in the body that protects you from germs, like bacteria and viruses that cause diseases. Through a series of steps called the immune response, the immune system learns how to recognize germs in order to fight them if your child is exposed to them in the future.

Your child is exposed to thousands of germs daily at home, at daycare or in the grocery store. Even a sweet kiss from a brother or sister can be full of germs. Most of these germs are harmless and are easily handled by your child's immune system. But some germs can make your child very sick.

Thanks to vaccination, your child's immune system learns how to recognize harmful germs. Vaccines help your child to develop the necessary defenses to fight disease, and to stay healthy!

HOW DO *VACCINES* WORK?

The dead or weakened germs in vaccines help your child's immune system to make two important tools: antibodies and immune memory. Together, these tools will help your child recognize and fight off the germs if exposed to them in the future.

Most children are fully protected after they are vaccinated. This means that they will never get serious vaccine-preventable diseases.

In rare cases, children who are immunized can still get the disease because they only get partial protection from the vaccine. This is more common in children with a health problem that affects their immune system. They may develop mild symptoms if they are exposed to a disease, but will not suffer serious complications.

It's just like...seatbelts are not 100% effective at protecting you while driving, but they significantly reduce your risk of being injured.

Did you know?
The word "immunization" comes from the word "immune," which means "protected from disease."

HOW ARE *VACCINES* GIVEN?

Most vaccines are given by an injection (a needle) into your child's upper arm or thigh. Some vaccines can be given orally (by mouth) or nasally (sprayed into the nose).

Your child can safely get more than one vaccine at a time. Some vaccines protect against several diseases in a single shot, while others are given separately.

WHAT IF MY CHILD CAN'T BE *VACCINATED?*

Some children cannot receive certain vaccines due to allergic reactions or other medical conditions. Because they can't be vaccinated, they are at risk of getting diseases that the vaccine would have protected them from.

You can help protect your children by encouraging those around your child to be up-to-date with their vaccination. Diseases that may not seem serious to adults can be very harmful to vulnerable children.

DISEASES PREVENTED BY ROUTINE *VACCINATIONS*

Vaccinating your children protects them from many vaccine-preventable diseases.

Nearly all these diseases can spread easily from person to person, mainly through coughing and sneezing. They can be serious enough to cause severe complications or even death. Getting your children vaccinated on time gives them the protection they need to stay healthy.

Did you know?
Your children, like you, should be vaccinated before you travel with them. They may need special vaccinations or need to be vaccinated earlier than usual.

DISEASES PREVENTED BY ROUTINE *VACCINATIONS*

Diseases	**Symptoms**	**Possible complications**
Diphtheria	1. Severe sore throat 2. High fever "	• Breathing and heart problems • Paralysis Death
Pertussis (Whooping cough)	• Violent coughing fits that may last for months • Difficulty eating, drinking, and breathing "	• Pneumonia • Convulsions • Brain damage • Death

DISEASES PREVENTED BY ROUTINE *VACCINATIONS (CONTIUNED)*

Tetanus	• Jaw spasms • Vocal cord spasms • Full-body muscle spasms	• Death
Polio	• Fever • Nausea and vomiting • General discomfort	• Breathing problems • Paralysis of arms and legs • Death
Haemophilus Influenzae Type b infections	• Severe swelling of the throat	• Deafness • Developmental delays • Pneumonia • Meningitis *(infection of the lining of the brain and spinal cord)* • Death
Mumps	• Fever • Headache • Swollen glands near jawbone	• Meningitis *(infection of the lining of the brain and spinal cord)* • Deafness • Infertility
Rubella	• Rash • Swollen glands	• Arthritis • Miscarriage • Malformations in an infant whose mother contracted rubella during pregnancy
Varicella (Chickenpox)	• Fever • Many small blisters that develop scabs • Itching	• Pneumonia • Encephalitis *(brain infection)* • Malformations in an infant whose mother contracted chickenpox during pregnancy • Death

DISEASES PREVENTED BY ROUTINE *VACCINATIONS (CONTIUNED)*

Meningococcal infection	• High fever • Severe headache • Nausea and vomiting • Red marks or tiny pin-size bruises on the skin • Blood infection	• Brain damage • Amputation of hands or feet • Death
Pneumococcal infection	• Ear and/or sinus infection • Blood infection	• Deafness • Brain damage • Pneumonia • Meningitis *(infection of the lining of the brain and spinal cord)* • Death
Hepatitis B	• Fever • Abdominal pain • Jaundice • Vomiting • Diarrhea	• Cirrhosis of the liver • Liver cancer • Death
Influenzae	• Fever • Cough • Fatigue • Headache • Muscle pain	• Ear and/or sinus infection • Bronchitis *(inflammation of the airways)* • Pneumonia • Death
Rotavirus	• High fever • Vomiting • Severe, watery diarrhea	• Severe dehydration • Death
Measles	• Rash • Cough • Fever Pink eye	• Pneumonia • Convulsions • Brain damag • Death

Visit Canada.ca/health to find out more about these and other vaccine-preventable diseases.

IF PEOPLE HARDLY EVER GET THESE DISEASES, WHY DOES MY CHILD NEED TO BE *VACCINATED*?

Diseases that were once common in childhood are now rare in Canada because of vaccines. But they still exist. Even one case of measles can spread quickly when people are not vaccinated. It is not easy to tell who is carrying the germ, or if your child has been exposed.

Many vaccine-preventable diseases have no treatment or cure. In some cases, children can die from complications of a disease. The best protection is to keep vaccinating.

To better explain the importance of vaccination, here is an analogy: It's just like when we started bailing out a boat that had a slow leak; the boat was full of water (full of diseases). We have been bailing (vaccinating) fast and hard, and now the boat is almost dry. If we stop bailing (vaccinating) the water will continue to come in as there is still a leak (infectious diseases are still present).

VACCINES ARE SAFE

Vaccines are safe and provide important benefits for your children's health throughout their lives.

Many parents with young children have not seen the vaccine-preventable diseases mentioned in this guide, so they may not know how serious the diseases are. As a result, parents may worry more about the side effects of vaccines than the diseases they prevent.

HOW ARE *VACCINES* APPROVED?

Like all medicines, vaccines need to go through a series of tests before they can be used in Canada. Several systems are in place to monitor the creation, the use and the safety of vaccines. Vaccine reactions are reported by healthcare providers to local public health authorities to make sure unusual or unexpected reactions can be dealt with quickly.

IS THE *VACCINE* SAFER THAN GETTING THE REAL DISEASE?

Yes. Your child's natural immune system has no problem handling the weak or dead germs in a vaccine. Your child may have a mild fever or a sore arm after vaccination but the se side effects only last a few days and should not disrupt daily activities.

However, if an unvaccinated child catches the real disease, the result can be serious, or even fatal. This is because active germs multiply quickly, and your child's immune system is not prepared to defend itself.

YOUR CHILD NEEDS TO BE *VACCINATED* ON TIME

Vaccines work best when they are given on time, beginning when your child is very young. Routine vaccination is free across Canada; however, schedules may differ in each province or territory.

Remember to check that your own vaccinations are up-to-date. Vaccination is a lifelong process.

Did you know?
Vaccination prevents between two and three million deaths worldwide every year. It is safe and simple, and it works!

WHY SHOULD I *VACCINATE* MY CHILD AT SUCH A YOUNG AGE?

The vaccination schedule is designed to protect your child before they are exposed to vaccine-preventable diseases. Children are immunized early in life because they are vulnerable to diseases and the consequences can be very serious. But if vaccinated on time, your child has the most protection as early as possible.

WHEN SHOULD MY CHILD BE *VACCINATED*?

Your child needs to be vaccinated at several stages in order to be fully protected. Some vaccines need to be given more than once to build up your child's immune system.

Immunization schedules could be different depending in which province or territory you live in. This means that some provinces or territories will give the same vaccine at different ages. But don't worry, your healthcare provider will give you a vaccination schedule that will tell you which vaccines are needed and at what age. Another way to find your child's immunization schedule is to check Canada.ca/health where the schedule for each province and territory is listed.

CAN MY CHILD GET MORE THAN ONE *VACCINE* AT A TIME?

Yes. Some vaccines are given together to protect against several diseases at once. Your child's immune system is AMAZING! It can easily handle more than one vaccine at a time safely and effectively.

Your healthcare provider will let you know which vaccines your child needs at each visit.

WHERE DO I GET MY CHILD *VACCINATED*?

Contact your healthcare provider to find out where to get vaccinations. You can search your local phone book or the Internet for your nearest public health office (CLSC in Quebec).

WHAT IF WE MISSED A SHOT?

Life with young children can be very busy. You may not be able to make every vaccination appointment for your child. But it is important to get back on schedule.

You should book an appointment with your healthcare provider as soon as possible. They can help you figure out what vaccines your child has already had, and which ones are needed.

WHAT IF WE MOVE?

If you move to another province or territory, your child's vaccination schedule may change. Once you have moved, contact your new healthcare provider to find out which vaccines may be needed. Remember to take your child's immunization record to the appointment with you.

Did you know?
Babies have the capacity to produce up to one billion antibodies. As such, it is estimated that (theoretically) an average baby could handle up to 10,000 vaccines at one time without concern.

YOUR CHILD DEPENDS ON YOU FOR *VACCINATION* PROTECTION

Getting your children vaccinated on time is one of the most important jobs you have as a parent. When you vaccinate your children, you protect them from serious diseases for the rest of their life.

WHY IS IT IMPORTANT TO KEEP TRACK OF YOUR CHILD'S *VACCINATION*?

Proof of vaccination may be requested. In some parts of Canada, children need to have all of their vaccinations up-to-date before starting school or daycare. This is needed to help prevent the spread of serious diseases in these settings.

Also, your child's vaccination history is helpful if you ever need to take your child to see another health-care provider or travel outside of Canada.

HOW DO I KEEP TRACK OF MY CHILD'S *VACCINATION*?

You will be given a vaccination record (card or booklet) with your child's recommended schedule at your first clinic visit. If your healthcare provider forgets, be sure to ask for one. It is important to bring this record with you every time you visit a healthcare provider. This is to make sure that it can be updated each time your child receives a vaccine.

You might find it helpful to use the checklist at the back of this guide, or download the ImmunizeCA app to help you keep track of your family's vaccinations.

ARE YOU TRAVELING?

When traveling to another country, you and your family may be at risk for vaccine-preventable diseases. These may include diseases for which vaccines are not routinely given in Canada. It is important to consult a healthcare provider, or visit a travel health clinic, at least six weeks before you travel. Certain vaccines may be recommended depending on your age, where you plan to travel and what you plan to do.

WHAT TO EXPECT AT YOUR CHILD'S FIRST ***VACCINATION***

You can help your child have a positive vaccination experience. Understanding what will happen when your child is vaccinated can make it easier on both of you.

WHAT IF MY CHILD HAS A COLD OR FEVER?

If your child is sick or has a fever when it's time for their vaccination, talk to your healthcare provider. They can assess whether it is okay to give the vaccination or if it is better to wait until your child is no longer sick.

BEFORE THE *VACCINATION*

Remember to take your child's vaccination record with you when you visit your healthcare provider or public health office (CLSC in Quebec). If you don't have a vaccination record, be sure to ask for one.

DURING THE *VACCINATION*

Your healthcare provider may ask you a few questions about your child's health, such as if they have allergies or health problems.

Here are some things you can do to help your child during the vaccination.

- **Relax.** Your child may react to your emotions. When you relax and stay positive, your child will be happier too.
- **Cuddle.** Hold and talk to your child during the vaccination. Studies have found that children who are held while getting a needle cry less.
- **Breastfeed.** If you are breastfeeding, try nursing your baby right before, during or after the needle. This will be comforting to your baby.

- **Distract.** Your gentle, soothing voice or touch can help comfort your baby. So can a favourite toy, telling a story or singing.

AFTER THE *VACCINATION*

Most children are fine after vaccination. Your child may have no reaction at all to the vaccine. In some cases, your child may:

- be fussy;
- be sleepier than usual;
- have a low fever; or
- have a sore, swollen, or red spot where the needle went in.

These reactions are normal and usually last between 12 and 24 hours. You can give your child medicine to help with the pain or lower the fever. Ask your healthcare provider what medicine is best.

BEFORE YOU GO HOME

Make an appointment for your child's next vaccination.

You will be asked to wait at the clinic for 15 to 20 minutes after your child's vaccination. This is because, as with any medicine, there is a very slight chance of a serious allergic reaction (anaphylaxis).

Signs of a serious allergic reaction include:

- breathing problems (wheezing);
- swelling of the face; and/or
- blotchy skin on the body (hives).

If you see any of these symptoms, talk to a healthcare provider immediately. They know what to do to counter the allergic reaction.

WHEN TO CALL YOUR HEALTHCARE PROVIDER

Serious reactions to vaccines are very rare. Call your healthcare provider or public health office (CLSC in Quebec) if your child has unusual symptoms after vaccination.

Unusual symptoms may include:

- a fever above 40°C (104°F);
- crying or fussing for more than 24 hours;
- worsening swelling where the needle went in;
- or unusual sleepiness.

You know your child best. If you notice anything that is not normal after a vaccination, check with your healthcare provider.

WHERE TO FIND MORE INFORMATION

It is important to get the facts about vaccination from reliable sources. Talk to a trusted healthcare provider about your child's vaccinations. This can be your doctor, nurse, or pharmacist.

Here are some websites you can trust to find information on vaccination:

- Public Health Agency of Canada
- Canadian Paediatric Society
- Immunize Canada

CHECKLIST FOR YOUR CHILD'S VACCINATIONS

- **Make an appointment.** The first vaccination may start at birth but certainly by the age of two months. Your healthcare provider will give you a schedule for your child.
- **Bring your child's vaccination record.** You will get this at your first appointment.
- **Make the next appointment.** Set a date for your child's next vaccination before you leave your healthcare provider.
- **Mark the next date in your cell phone or home calendar.** Do this as soon as possible so you will not forget.

Keep your child's vaccination record in a safe place, so you can find it when you need it. Remember, vaccination is part of your children's routine care. Keeping vaccinations up-to-date is important to protect their health.

1. How does it help a person to have the basic information about vaccination summarized?
2. What other questions might a person have about vaccination?

"COUNCIL CONCLUSIONS ON VACCINATIONS AS AN EFFECTIVE TOOL IN PUBLIC HEALTH," BY THE COUNCIL OF THE EUROPEAN UNION, FROM THE EMPLOYMENT, SOCIAL POLICY, HEALTH AND CONSUMER AFFAIRS COUNCIL MEETING IN BRUSSELS, DECEMBER 1, 2014

The Council adopted the following conclusions:

"The Council of the European Union

1. RECALLS that under Article 168 of the Treaty on the Functioning of the European Union (TFEU), Union action, which shall complement national policies, shall cover the fight against the major health scourges by promoting research into their causes, their transmission and their prevention, as well as health information and education, and monitoring, early warning of and combating serious cross-border threats to health. The Union shall encourage cooperation between the Member States and, if necessary, lend support to their action. Union action shall respect the responsibilities of the Member States for the definition of their health policy and for the organisation and delivery of health services and medical care.

2. RECALLS Regulation (EC) No 851/2004 of the European Parliament and of the Council of 21 April 2004 establishing a European Centre for Disease Prevention and Control (ECDC). The ECDC supports activities for the prevention and control

of communicable diseases: epidemiological surveillance, risk assessment training programmes and rapid alert and response mechanisms, and should undertake activities to ensure that Member States regularly exchange good practices and experiences on vaccination programmes.

3. RECALLS Decision No 1082/2013/EU of the European Parliament and of the Council of 22 October 2013, on serious cross-border threats to health and repealing Decision No 2119/98/CE, which provides that Member States shall consult each other in liaison with the Commission through the Health Security Committee with a view to coordinating their response to serious cross-border threats to health, including communicable diseases. It also provides for a possibility to engage in the joint procurement of medical countermeasures on a voluntary basis.

4. RECALLS the third Programme for the Union action in the field of health (2014-2020) established by Regulation (EU) No 282/2014, aiming to support capacity-building against major cross-border health threats and, to develop preparedness and response planning, taking into account complementarity with the work programme of the ECDC in the fight against communicable diseases.

5. RECALLS Council Recommendation on seasonal influenza vaccination (2009/1019/EU) which encourages the Member States to adopt and implement national, regional or local action plans or policies aimed at improving seasonal influenza vaccination coverage, with the aim of achieving 75% coverage in the risk groups by 2015.

6. RECALLS the Council conclusions on childhood immunisation (2011/C 202/02), in which the Member States and the Commission are invited, inter alia, to share experiences and best practices to improve the vaccination coverage of children against vaccine-preventable diseases;

7. POINTS OUT that vaccines are medicinal products subject to the rules and procedures adopted at Union level, authorised by national authorities or by the Commission on the basis of an assessment carried out by the European Medicines Agency and subject to postmarketing monitoring.

8. RECALLS the European Region Vaccine Action Plan 2015 to 2020 of the World Health Organisation (WHO), which was approved in response to the Decade of Vaccines, setting a course through a regional vision and goals for immunisation and control of vaccine-preventable diseases from 2015 to 2020 and beyond, by defining priority action areas, indicators and targets, while taking into account the specific needs and challenges of countries in the European region.

9. POINTS out that post-marketing studies including those carried out by marketing authorisation holders are important for the evaluation of vaccine products and should be carried out in a transparent way. Studies on the impact of vaccination programmes, carried out independently from commercial interests are equally important. Both kinds of studies can contribute to increasing public trust in immunisation. Member States are encouraged to fund independent studies.

10. RECOGNISES that communicable diseases, including some re-emerging ones, such as tuberculosis, measles, pertussis and rubella, still present a public health challenge and can cause a high number of infections and deaths, and that the recent emergence and outbreaks of communicable diseases, such as polio, avian influenza H5N1 and H7N9, Middle East respiratory syndrome caused by a coronavirus (MERS) and Ebola virus disease have confirmed that vigilance must remain high also with respect to diseases that are not currently present in the territory of the Union.

11. RECOGNISES that while vaccination programmes are the responsibility of individual Member States and that various vaccination schemes exist in the EU, efforts to improve vaccination coverage may also benefit from cooperation within the EU and from improved synergies with other EU policy areas, having special regard to the most vulnerable populations identified in the different regions and individual Member States of the Union and to increasing mobility.

12. OBSERVES that many vaccines used in community vaccination programmes have been able to prevent disease in individuals and at the same time interrupt the circulation of pathogens through the so called "herd immunity" phenomenon, contributing to a healthier global society. Community immunity could thus be considered an objective in national vaccination plans.

13. CONSIDERS that an evidence-based, cost-effective, safe and efficient immunisation system is an integral part of a well-functioning health system.

14. POINTS OUT that, given the changes in the demographic structure of the European population, there must be a greater focus on preventing infectious diseases by means of vaccination of all age groups where this improves the epidemiological control of the disease.

15. RECOGNISES that immunisation programmes require sustainable access to long-term funding and quality supply.

16. RECOGNISES the importance of the general public understanding the value of vaccinations and NOTES that the occasional lack of awareness of the benefits of some vaccines and the increasing refusal of vaccination in some Member States may lead to under-vaccination in some populations, resulting in public health problems and costly outbreaks.

17. RECOGNISES that the public should be aware of the value of vaccination and UNDERLINES the crucial role of health care professionals in informing and educating the population about the benefits of vaccination.

18. RECOGNISES that effective vaccination campaigns are useful in preventing the spread of communicable diseases that may cause permanent health damage or even death, particularly in vulnerable age-groups of the population.

19. RECOGNISES the positive effect that a reinforced vaccination policy at national level may have on the development of and research in new vaccines in the EU.

20. POINTS OUT that Member States should, if relevant, inform their citizens travelling abroad about the risk of communicable diseases which are not present in the Union, but may be contracted on international trips outside the Union.

21. POINTS OUT that some viral agents may also cause chronic pathologies, some of a neoplastic nature, such as cervical cancer, and that vaccinations could contribute to addressing these diseases.

22. CONSIDERS IT NECESSARY that an analysis and evaluation of the safety, effectiveness and impact of vaccines to prevent distinct communicable diseases, of the risks related to communicable diseases and of the usefulness of vaccinations is periodically carried out in the European Union on the basis of developments in scientific knowledge.

23. CONSIDERS IT USEFUL that Member States collaborate and exchange best practices concerning the prevention of communicable diseases through vaccination given the fact that communicable diseases cannot be confined to one country either within or outside the European Union, and to do so with the support of the ECDC and the WHO.

24. CONSIDERS IT NECESSARY that policies to encourage research, including clinical and, post-authorisation studies in the field of vaccination, be supported within the Union, taking into account also the financial constraints, in order to make safer and more effective vaccines available.

25. OBSERVES that as a result of the success in reducing the spread of a number of serious communicable diseases due to the widespread use of vaccinations, the population may believe that these diseases no longer represent a threat to public health.

26. CONSIDERS IT APPROPRIATE, especially in order to react to inaccurate information regarding vaccinations in some Member States, that communication campaigns continue to be carried out to educate the public about the risks related to communicable diseases preventable by vaccination.

27. CONSIDERS IT USEFUL to consult stakeholders including health professionals´ organisations, academia, industry and civil society to give them the opportunity to express their positions which could be of use Member States' authorities.

28. Invites MEMBER STATES to:

a) continue to improve epidemiological surveillance and evaluation of the situation concerning communicable diseases in their territories, including diseases preventable by vaccination;

b) continue to improve national vaccination programmes and to strengthen national capacity for carrying out evidence-based, cost-effective vaccination, including the introduction of new vaccines where considered appropriate;

c) continue to develop plans and standard operating procedures in collaboration with the ECDC and the WHO to ensure a timely and effective response to vaccine-preventable diseases during outbreaks, humanitarian crises and emergencies;

d) continue to develop comprehensive and coordinated approaches within vaccination programmes, following the Health in All Policies approach creating synergies with broader health policies and pro-actively working with other preventive sectors;

e) ensure transparency with regard to the post-marketing evaluations of vaccines and of studies on the impact of vaccination programmes in order to provide reliable information for both governments, medicines regulators and manufacturers;

f) actively offer appropriate vaccination to population groups considered to be at risk in terms of specific diseases and consider immunization beyond infancy and early childhood by creating vaccination programmes with life-long approach;

g) work with health professionals on risk communication in order to maximize their role in informed decision making;

h) further increase activities aimed at expanding, where necessary, the immunology and vaccinology components of the basic medical training curricula for students of medical and health sciences and provide health professionals with relevant in-services training opportunities;

i) inform the population in order to raise its trust in vaccinations programmes, using appropriate tools and communication campaigns also by engaging opinion leaders, civil society and relevant stakeholders (e.g. academia).

29. Invites MEMBER STATES and the COMMISSION to:

a) continue to exchange information and data with the ECDC and the WHO on the risks posed by communicable diseases and on national vaccination policies; in this regard, the communication toolkits developed by the ECDC and made available to the Member States (following the example of the already developed toolkit for influenza) could be taken into consideration;

b) continue to exchange data on vaccination coverage for all target risk groups;

c) convey informed and clear messages on vaccinations;

d) find the best ways to allow stakeholders, including industry and civil society, to express their positions;

e) promote activities aimed at engaging with health care professionals more directly and actively on critical vaccination issues, in particular focused on strengthening their role in advocating vaccination;

f) share information on cost-effectiveness studies in the EU for the implementation of new vaccines, which would assist the Member States in their national vaccination programmes;

g) coordinate activities aimed at advocating and encouraging the use of vaccines included in national vaccination programmes by sharing information on communication plans and campaigns for vaccine introduction;

h) further encourage research and innovation aimed at developing of new vaccines and demonstrating the benefits of a life course approach, the cost effectiveness of immunisation and the effectiveness of risk communication, while at all times giving priority to citizens' safety;

i) develop joint action programmes co-financed by the Commission and Member States to share best practices on national vaccination policies;

j) encourage research activities and continue to exchange information in respect of the monitoring of vaccination impact on disease burden and the development of new vaccines.

30. Invites the COMMISSION to:

a) identify and encourage synergy between the promotion of immunisation and the implementation of relevant EU legislation and policies, in particular focusing on the identification and development of integrative and coherent approaches for better preparedness and coordination in health emergencies, while fully respecting national competences;

b) ensure that European Union funding is channeled to foster current and future vaccine research, including wide partnership between academia, industry, and public and private funders, and to address and resolve bottlenecks in vaccine development;

c) ensure that funding provided by the European Union and other stakeholders, such as academia or public health institutions, and made available by the relevant public health bodies is channeled to support post-marketing studies, including studies on vaccine effectiveness and the impact of immunisation programs carried out by national public health institutes, academia and other partnerships;

d) examine with the ECDC and the EMA and in close cooperation with the WHO, options to:

- identify guidance and methodologies which Member States could choose to use on a voluntary basis to strengthen the financial and programmatic consistency and sustainability of their national vaccination programmes and the cost effectiveness of vaccines;
- facilitate the introduction of research methods which Member States could use voluntarily to assess the effectiveness of risk communication and the dynamics of social attitudes towards vaccines and devise effective strategies to promote vaccine uptake;

e) assist Member States in making the best use of the technical and scientific expertise of the Union agencies and Commission´s technical committees, in order to respond to questions;

f) place technological and IT tools at the disposal of Member States and improve links to existing European portals and tools to support Member States in their efforts to strengthen vaccination as an effective tool in public health."

1. How is disease control a personal issue, and how is it a community issue?
2. How big is a "community" when it comes to disease control?

"CALIFORNIA SENATE BILL NO. 277," APPROVED JUNE 30, 2015

An act to amend Sections 120325, 120335, 120370, and 120375 of, to add Section 120338 to, and to repeal Section 120365 of, the Health and Safety Code, relating to public health.

[Approved by Governor June 30, 2015. Filed with Secretary of State June 30, 2015.]

LEGISLATIVE COUNSEL'S DIGEST

SB 277, Pan. Public health: vaccinations.

Existing law prohibits the governing authority of a school or other institution from unconditionally admitting any person as a pupil of any public or private elementary or secondary school, child care center, day nursery, nursery school, family day care home, or development center, unless prior to his or her admission to that institution he or she has been fully immunized against various diseases, including measles, mumps, and pertussis, subject to any specific age criteria. Existing law authorizes an exemption from those provisions for medical reasons or because of personal beliefs, if specified forms are submitted to the governing authority. Existing law requires the governing authority of a school or other institution to require documentary proof of each entrant's immunization status. Existing law authorizes the governing authority of a school or other institution to temporarily exclude a child from the school or institution if the authority has good cause to believe that the child has been exposed to one of those diseases, as specified.

This bill would eliminate the exemption from existing specified immunization requirements based upon personal beliefs, but would allow exemption from future immunization requirements deemed appropriate by the State Department of Public Health for either medical reasons or personal beliefs. The bill would exempt pupils in a home-based private school and students enrolled in an independent study program and who do not receive classroom-based instruction, pursuant to specified law from the prohibition described above. The bill would allow pupils who, prior to January 1, 2016, have a letter or affidavit on file at a private or public elementary or secondary school, child day care center, day nursery, nursery school, family day care home, or development center stating beliefs opposed to immunization, to be enrolled in any private or public elementary or secondary school, child day care center, day nursery, nursery school, family day care home, or development center within the state until the pupil enrolls in the next grade span, as defined. Except as under the circumstances described above, on and after July 1, 2016, the bill would prohibit a governing authority from unconditionally admitting to any of those institutions for the first time or admitting or advancing any pupil to the 7th grade level, unless the pupil has been immunized as required by the bill. The bill would specify that its provisions do not prohibit a pupil who qualifies for an individualized education program, pursuant to specified laws, from accessing any special education and related services required by his or her individualized education program. The bill would narrow the authorization for temporary exclusion from a school or other institution to make it applicable only to a child who has been exposed to a specified disease and whose documentary proof of immunization status does not show proof of immunization against one of the diseases described above. The bill would make conforming changes to related provisions.

Vote: majority Appropriation: no Fiscal Committee: no Local Program: no

THE PEOPLE OF THE STATE OF CALIFORNIA DO ENACT AS FOLLOWS:

SECTION 1. Section 120325 of the Health and Safety Code is amended to read:
120325. In enacting this chapter, but excluding Section 120380, and in enacting Sections 120400, 120405, 120410, and 120415, it is the intent of the Legislature to provide:

(a) A means for the eventual achievement of total immunization of appropriate age groups against the following childhood diseases:
(1) Diphtheria.
(2) Hepatitis B.
(3) Haemophilus influenzae type b.
(4) Measles.
(5) Mumps.
(6) Pertussis (whooping cough).
(7) Poliomyelitis.

(8) Rubella.
(9) Tetanus.
(10) Varicella (chickenpox).
(11) Any other disease deemed appropriate by the department, taking into consideration the recommendations of the Advisory Committee on Immunization Practices of the United States Department of Health and Human Services, the American Academy of Pediatrics, and the American Academy of Family Physicians.
(b) That the persons required to be immunized be allowed to obtain immunizations from whatever medical source they so desire, subject only to the condition that the immunization be performed in accordance with the regulations of the department and that a record of the immunization is made in accordance with the regulations.
(c) Exemptions from immunization for medical reasons.
(d) For the keeping of adequate records of immunization so that health departments, schools, and other institutions, parents or guardians, and the persons immunized will be able to ascertain that a child is fully or only partially immunized, and so that appropriate public agencies will be able to ascertain the immunization needs of groups of children in schools or other institutions.
(e) Incentives to public health authorities to design innovative and creative programs that will promote and achieve full and timely immunization of children.

SEC. 2. Section 120335 of the Health and Safety Code is amended to read:

120335. (a) As used in this chapter, "governing authority" means the governing board of each school district or the authority of each other private or public institution responsible for the operation and control of the institution or the principal or administrator of each school or institution.

(b) The governing authority shall not unconditionally admit any person as a pupil of any private or public elementary or secondary school, child care center, day nursery, nursery school, family day care home, or development center, unless, prior to his or her first admission to that institution, he or she has been fully immunized. The following are the diseases for which immunizations shall be documented:

(1) Diphtheria.

(2) Haemophilus influenzae type b.

(3) Measles.

(4) Mumps.

(5) Pertussis (whooping cough).

(6) Poliomyelitis.

(7) Rubella.

(8) Tetanus.

(9) Hepatitis B.

(10) Varicella (chickenpox).

(11) Any other disease deemed appropriate by the department, taking into consideration the recommendations of the Advisory Committee on Immunization Practices of the United States Department of Health and Human Services, the American Academy of Pediatrics, and the American Academy of Family Physicians.

(c) Notwithstanding subdivision (b), full immunization against hepatitis B shall not be a condition by which the governing authority shall admit or advance any pupil to the 7th grade level of any private or public elementary or secondary school.

(d) The governing authority shall not unconditionally admit or advance any pupil to the 7th grade level of any private or public elementary or secondary school unless the pupil has been fully immunized against pertussis, including all pertussis boosters appropriate for the pupil's age.

(e) The department may specify the immunizing agents that may be utilized and the manner in which immunizations are administered.

(f) This section does not apply to a pupil in a home-based private school or a pupil who is enrolled in an independent study program pursuant to Article 5.5 (commencing with Section 51745) of Chapter 5 of Part 28 of the Education Code and does not receive classroom-based instruction.

(g) (1) A pupil who, prior to January 1, 2016, submitted a letter or affidavit on file at a private or public elementary or secondary school, child day care center, day nursery, nursery school, family day care home, or development center stating beliefs opposed to immunization shall be allowed enrollment to any private or public elementary or secondary school, child day care center, day nursery, nursery school, family day care home, or development center within the state until the pupil enrolls in the next grade span.

(2) For purposes of this subdivision, "grade span" means each of the following:

(A) Birth to preschool.

(B) Kindergarten and grades 1 to 6, inclusive,

including transitional kindergarten.

(C) Grades 7 to 12, inclusive.

(3) Except as provided in this subdivision, on and after July 1, 2016, the governing authority shall not unconditionally admit to any of those institutions specified in this subdivision for the first time, or admit or advance any pupil to 7th grade level, unless the pupil has been immunized for his or her age as required by this section.

(h) This section does not prohibit a pupil who qualifies for an individualized education program, pursuant to federal law and Section 56026 of the Education Code, from accessing any special education and related services required by his or her individualized education program.

SEC. 3. Section 120338 is added to the Health and Safety Code, to read:

120338. Notwithstanding Sections 120325 and 120335, any immunizations deemed appropriate by the department pursuant to paragraph (11) of subdivision (a) of Section 120325 or paragraph (11) of subdivision (b) of Section 120335, may be mandated before a pupil's first admission to any private or public elementary or secondary school, child care center, day nursery, nursery school, family day care home, or development center, only if exemptions are allowed for both medical reasons and personal beliefs.

SEC. 4. Section 120365 of the Health and Safety Code is repealed.

SEC. 5. Section 120370 of the Health and Safety Code is amended to read:

120370. (a) If the parent or guardian files with the governing authority a written statement by a licensed physician to the effect that the physical condition of the child is such, or medical circumstances relating to the child are such, that immunization is not considered safe, indicating the specific nature and probable duration of the medical condition or circumstances, including, but not limited to, family medical history, for which the physician does not recommend immunization, that child shall be exempt from the requirements of Chapter 1 (commencing with Section 120325, but excluding Section 120380) and Sections 120400, 120405, 120410, and 120415 to the extent indicated by the physician's statement.

(b) If there is good cause to believe that a child has been exposed to a disease listed in subdivision (b) of Section 120335 and his or her documentary proof of immunization status does not show proof of immunization against that disease, that child may be temporarily excluded from the school or institution until the local health officer is satisfied that the child is no longer at risk of developing or transmitting the disease.

SEC. 6. Section 120375 of the Health and Safety Code is amended to read:

120375. (a) The governing authority of each school or institution included in Section 120335 shall require documentary proof of each entrant's immunization status. The governing authority shall record the immunizations of each new entrant in the entrant's permanent enrollment and scholarship record on a form provided by the department. The immunization record of each new entrant admitted conditionally shall be reviewed periodically by the governing authority to ensure that within the time periods designated by regulation of the department he or she has been fully immunized against all of the diseases listed in Section 120335, and immunizations received subsequent to entry shall be added to the pupil's immunization record.

(b) The governing authority of each school or institution included in Section 120335 shall prohibit from further attendance any pupil admitted conditionally who failed to obtain the required immunizations within the time limits allowed in the regulations of the department, unless the pupil is exempted under Section 120370, until that pupil has been fully immunized against all of the diseases listed in Section 120335.

(c) The governing authority shall file a written report on the immunization status of new entrants to the school or institution under their jurisdiction with the department and the local health department at times and on forms prescribed by the department. As provided in paragraph (4) of subdivision (a) of Section 49076 of the Education Code, the local health department shall have access to the complete health information as it relates to immunization of each student in the schools or other institutions listed in Section 120335 in order to determine immunization deficiencies.

(d) The governing authority shall cooperate with the county health officer in carrying out programs for the immunization of persons applying for admission to any school or institution under its jurisdiction. The governing board of any school district may use funds, property, and personnel of the district for that purpose. The governing authority of any school or other institution may permit any licensed physician or any qualified registered nurse as provided in Section 2727.3 of the Business and Professions Code to administer immunizing agents to any person seeking admission to any school or institution under its jurisdiction.

1. Do you think that parents should have the right to decide not to vaccinate their children due to their own personal or religious beliefs?

CHAPTER 3

WHAT THE COURTS SAY

Since vaccination was invented to control the spread of smallpox, courts in Western countries have ruled on cases involving vaccination regulations. Some laws make vaccination against certain diseases not only required but easily available and without charge. Laws in North America and Europe recognize the right to refuse vaccination because of conscience. This moral exemption is usually intended to respect religious rights, but in the United States, some schools and doctors have interpreted it to allow parents to refuse immunization due to fears of vaccine injuries. When such refusals are not allowed, a person can sue the private school or government authority, and the courts decide how the law applies.

Four times a year, the US Department of Justice sends a report to the Advisory Commission on Childhood Vaccines, stating the number of settlements on vaccine injuries and deaths. People who claim an injury or death due to a vaccine cannot sue the manufacturer. Instead, the federal government must be sued, leading to the possibility of a settlement through the National Vaccine Injury Compensation Program.

EXCERPT FROM *JACOBSON V. MASSACHUSETTS*, 197 US 11 (1905), US SUPREME COURT DECISION, DECIDED FEBRUARY 20, 1905

MR. JUSTICE HARLAN, after making the foregoing statement, delivered the opinion of the court. [...]

According to settled principles the police power of a State must be held to embrace, at least, such reasonable regulations established directly by legislative enactment as will protect the public health and the public safety. [...]

The defendant insists that his liberty is invaded when the State subjects him to fine or imprisonment for neglecting or refusing to submit to vaccination; that a compulsory vaccination law is unreasonable, arbitrary and oppressive, and, therefore, hostile to the inherent right of every freeman to care for his own body and health in such was as to him seems best and that the execution of such a law against one who objects to vaccination, no matter for what reason, is nothing short of an assault upon his person. But the liberty secured by the Constitution of the United States to every person within its jurisdiction does not import an absolute right in each person to be, at all times and in all circumstances, wholly freed from restraint. There are manifold restraints to which every person is necessarily subject for the common good. [...] Real liberty for all could not exist under the operation of a principle which recognizes the right of each individual person to use his own, whether in respect of his person or his property, regardless of the injury that may be done to others. [...]

Applying these principles to the present case, it is to be observed that the legislature of Massachusetts required the inhabitants of a city or town to be vaccinated only when, in the opinion of the Board of Health, that was necessary for the public health or the public safety. [...] Upon the principle of self-defense, of paramount necessity, a community has the right to protect itself against an epidemic of disease which threatens the safety of its members. It is to be observed that when the regulation in question was adopted, smallpox, according to the recitals in the regulation adopted by the Board of Health, was prevalent to some extent in the city of Cambridge and the disease was increasing. If such was the situation -- and nothing is asserted or appears in the record to the contrary -- if we are to attach any value whatever to the knowledge which, it is safe to affirm, is common to all civilized peoples touching smallpox and the methods most usually employed to eradicate that disease, it cannot be adjudged that the present regulation of the Board of Health was not necessary in order to protect the public health and secure the public safety. Smallpox being prevalent and increasing at Cambridge, the court would usurp the functions of another branch of government if it adjudged, as matter of law, that the mode adopted under the sanction of the State, to protect the people at large was arbitrary and not justified by the necessities of the case. We say necessities of the case because it might be that an acknowledged power of a local community to protect itself against an epidemic threatening the safety of all, might be exercised in particular circumstances and in reference to particular persons in such an arbitrary, unreasonable manner, or might go so far beyond what was reasonably required for the safety of the public, as to authorize or compel the courts to interfere for the protection of such persons. [...] If the mode adopted by the Commonwealth of Massachusetts for the protection of its local communities against smallpox proved to be distressing, inconvenient or objectionable to some -- if nothing more could be reasonably affirmed of the statute in question -- the answer is that it was the duty of the constituted authorities primarily to keep in view the welfare, comfort and safety of the many, and not permit the interests of the many to be subordinated to the wishes or convenience of the few. There is, of course, a sphere within which the individual may assert the supremacy of his own will and rightfully dispute the authority of any human government. But it is equally true that in every well-ordered society charged with the duty of conserving the safety of its members the rights of the individual in respect of his liberty may at times, under the pressure of great dangers, be subjected to such restraint, to be enforced by reasonable regulations, as the safety of the general public may demand. An American citizen, arriving at an American port on a vessel in which, during the voyage, there had been cases of yellow fever or Asiatic cholera, although apparently free from disease himself, may yet, in some circumstances, be held in quarantine against his will on board of such vessel or in a quarantine station until it be ascertained by inspection, conducted with due diligence, that the danger of the spread of the disease among the community at large has disappeared. [...]

Before closing this opinion we deem it appropriate, in order to prevent misapprehension as to our views, to observe -- perhaps to repeat a thought already sufficiently expressed, namely -- that the police power of a State, whether exercised by the legislature, or by a local body acting under its authority, may be exerted in such circumstances or by regulations so arbitrary and oppressive in particular cases as to justify the interference of the courts to prevent wrong and oppression. Extreme cases can be readily suggested. Ordinarily such cases are not safe guides in the administration of the law. It is easy, for instance, to suppose the case of an adult who is embraced by the mere words of the act, but yet to subject whom to vaccination in a particular condition of his health or body, would be cruel and inhuman in the last degree. We are not to be understood as holding that the statute was intended to be applied to such a case, or, if it was so intended, that the judiciary would not be competent to interfere and protect the health and life of the individual concerned. [...]

Until otherwise informed by the highest court of Massachusetts we are not inclined to hold that the statute establishes the absolute rule that an adult must be vaccinated if it be apparent or can be shown with reasonable certainty that he is not at the time a fit subject of vaccination or that vaccination, by reason of his then condition, would seriously impair his health or probably cause his death. No such case is here presented. It is the case of an adult who, for aught that appears, was himself in perfect health and a fit subject of vaccination, and yet, while remaining in the community, refused to obey the statute and the regulation adopted in execution of its provisions for the protection of the public health and the public safety, confessedly endangered by the presence of a dangerous disease.

We now decide only that the statute covers the present case, and that nothing clearly appears that would justify this court in holding it to be unconstitutional and inoperative in its application to the plaintiff in error.

The judgment of the court below must be affirmed.

It is so ordered.

1. How does this court ruling concerning smallpox vaccination law in 1905 relate to present-day mandatory vaccination programs?

"*PHILLIPS V. CITY OF NEW YORK*," UNITED STATES COURT OF APPEALS FOR THE SECOND CIRCUIT, DECIDED JANUARY 7, 2015

NICOLE PHILLIPS, individually and on behalf of B.P. and S.P., minors,

DINA CHECK, on behalf of minor M.C.,

FABIAN MENDOZA-VACA, individually and on behalf of M.M. and V.M., minors,

Plaintiffs-Appellants,

— v. —

CITY OF NEW YORK, ERIC T. SCHNEIDERMAN, in his official capacity as Attorney General, State of New York, DR. NIRAV R. SHAH, in his official capacity as Commissioner, New York State Department of Health, NEW YORK CITY DEPARTMENT OF EDUCATION,

Defendants-Appellees.

B e f o r e:

LYNCH and CHIN, Circuit Judges, and KORMAN, *District Judge*. The Honorable Edward R. Korman, of the United States District Court for the Eastern District of New York, sitting by designation.

Plaintiffs-appellants challenge on constitutional grounds New York State's requirement that all children be vaccinated in order to attend public school. Plaintiffs-appellants argue that the statutory vaccination requirement, which is subject to medical and religious exemptions, violates their substantive due process rights, the Free Exercise Clause of the First Amendment, the Equal Protection Clause of the Fourteenth Amendment, the Ninth Amendment, and both state and municipal law. On the same grounds, plaintiffs-appellants argue that a state regulation permitting state officials to temporarily exclude students who are exempted from the vaccination requirement from school during an outbreak of a vaccine-preventable disease is unconstitutional. The district court concluded that the statute and regulation are constitutional. We agree and therefore AFFIRM.

PATRICIA FINN, Patricia Finn, Attorney, P.C., Piermont, New York, for *Plaintiffs-Appellants.*

JAMES ANDREW KENT, Assistant Solicitor General (Steven C. Wu, Deputy Solicitor General, *on the brief*) on *behalf* of Barbara D. Underwood, Solicitor General, for State *Defendants-Appellees.*

JANE L. GORDON on behalf of Zachary W. Carter, Corporation Counsel of the City of New York, for *Municipal Defendants-Appellees.*

PER CURIAM:

Plaintiffs brought this action challenging on constitutional grounds New York State's requirement that all children be vaccinated in order to attend public school. Plaintiffs argued that the statutory vaccination requirement, which is subject to medical and religious exemptions, violates their substantive due process rights, the Free Exercise Clause of the First Amendment, the Equal Protection Clause of the Fourteenth Amendment, the Ninth Amendment, and both state and municipal law. On the same grounds, plaintiffs argued that a state regulation permitting school officials to temporarily exclude from school students who are exempted from the vaccination requirement during an outbreak of a vaccine-preventable disease is unconstitutional. Defendants moved to dismiss or for summary judgment. The district court (William F. Kuntz II, *Judge*) granted defendants' motions. Because we conclude that the statute and regulation are a constitutionally permissible exercise of the State's police power and do not infringe on the free exercise of religion, and we determine that plaintiffs' remaining arguments are either meritless or waived, we affirm.

BACKGROUND

New York requires that students in the State's public schools be immunized against various vaccine-preventable illnesses. The New York Public Health Law provides that "[n]o principal, teacher, owner or person in charge of a school shall permit any child to be admitted to such school, or to attend such school, in excess of fourteen days" without a certificate of immunization. N.Y. Pub. Health Law § 2164(7)(a). The statute provides two exemptions from the immunization mandate. First, a medical exemption is available "[i]f any physician licensed to practice medicine in this state certifies that such immunization may be detrimental to a child's health." Id. § 2164(8). Second, the a religious exemption is available for "children whose parent, parents, or guardian hold genuine and sincere religious beliefs which are contrary to the practices herein required." Id. § 2164(9). The State provides multiple layers of review for parents if either of these exemptions is denied.

Plaintiffs Nicole Phillips and Fabian Mendoza-Vaca, who are Catholic, received religious exemptions for their children. In November 2011 and January 2012, however, the Phillips and Mendoza-Vaca children were excluded from school when a fellow student was diagnosed with chicken pox, pursuant to a state regulation that provides, "in the event of an outbreak ... of a vaccine-preventable disease in a school, the commissioner, or his or her designee, ... may order the appropriate school officials to exclude from attendance" those students who have received exemptions from mandatory vaccination. 10 N.Y.C.R.R. § 66-1.10.

Plaintiff Dina Check applied for a religious exemption for her daughter, M.C. After asking Check to clarify her basis for seeking the exemption, a Department of Education ("DOE") official ultimately denied the exemption, finding that Check's objections to vaccinating M.C. were not based on genuine and sincere religious beliefs. Check then brought this lawsuit seeking a preliminary injunction to compel the DOE to allow M.C. to attend school unvaccinated.

The district court (Sandra L. Townes, *Judge*) referred the preliminary injunction application to Magistrate Judge Lois Bloom, who held a hearing at which Check testified regarding the purported religious basis for her objections to vaccines. Check testified that she is Catholic and stated, "How I treat my daughter's health and her well-being is strictly by the word of God." (Joint App'x

136.) Check also testified, however, that she believed that vaccination "could hurt my daughter. It could kill her. It could put her into anaphylactic shock. It could cause any number of things." (Id. at 146.) On cross-examination, Check testified that she did not know of any tenets of Catholicism that prohibited vaccinations. She also detailed several adverse reactions that M.C. had had to vaccinations before Check determined not to subject her to any further inoculation, and stated that these bad reactions led Check to ask God for guidance and protection.

The Magistrate Judge issued a Report and Recommendation recommending that the request for a preliminary injunction be denied. She found that Check's testimony demonstrated that her views on vaccination were primarily health-related and did not constitute a genuine and sincere religious belief. The Magistrate Judge noted especially that "plaintiff's testimony that she did not adopt her views opposing vaccination until she believed that immunization jeopardized her daughter's health is compelling evidence that plaintiff's refusal to immunize her child is based on medical considerations and not religious beliefs." (Id. at 211.) The district court adopted the Report and Recommendation and denied injunctive relief.

Check's case was subsequently consolidated with the Phillips and Mendoza-Vaca cases before Judge Kuntz. Plaintiffs thereafter jointly filed an amended complaint, alleging that the State's mandatory vaccination requirement and the regulation permitting temporary exclusion of exempted schoolchildren during a disease outbreak were unconstitutional. Specifically, plaintiffs alleged that the statute and regulation violated the Free

Exercise Clause of the First Amendment, their rights to substantive due process under the Fourteenth Amendment, the Ninth Amendment, the Equal Protection Clause, and state and municipal law. The municipal defendants moved to dismiss or for summary judgment, and the State defendants moved to dismiss. The district court granted the motions on June 5, 2014. Phillips v. City of New York, Nos. 12-cv-98 (WFK)(LB), 12-cv-237 (WFK)(LB), 13-cv-791 (WFK)(LB), 2014 WL 2547584 (E.D.N.Y. June 5, 2014). Plaintiffs filed their Notice of Appeal five days later, on June 10, 2014. Nine days after that, plaintiffs moved for reconsideration in the district court. The district court denied the motion, holding that because plaintiffs had already filed their Notice of Appeal, it no longer had jurisdiction.

DISCUSSION

We review *de novo* the district court's grant of a motion to dismiss, accepting as true all facts alleged in the complaint and drawing all reasonable inferences in favor of the plaintiff. Kassner v. 2nd Ave. Delicatessen Inc., 496 F.3d 229, 237 (2d Cir. 2007).

I. Substantive Due Process

Plaintiffs argue that New York's mandatory vaccination requirement violates substantive due process. This argument is foreclosed by the Supreme Court's decision in Jacobson v. Commonwealth of Massachusetts, 197 U.S. 11(1905). In that case, the plaintiff challenged Massachusetts's compulsory vaccination law under the Fourteenth Amendment. The Supreme Court held that mandatory vaccination was within the State's police power. Id. at 25-27; see Zucht v. King, 260 U.S. 174, 176 (1922) ("Jacobson ... settled that it is within the police power of a state to provide for compulsory vaccination."). The Court rejected the claim that the individual liberty guaranteed by the Constitution overcame the State's judgment that mandatory vaccination was in the interest of the population as a whole. Jacobson, 197 U.S. at 38. Plaintiffs argue that a growing body of scientific evidence demonstrates that vaccines cause more harm to society than good, but as Jacobson made clear, that is a determination for the legislature, not the individual objectors. See id. at 37-38.5 Plaintiffs' substantive due process challenge to the mandatory vaccination regime is therefore no more compelling than Jacobson's was more than a century ago. See Caviezel v. Great Neck Pub. Schs., 500 F. App'x 16, 19 (2d Cir. 2012) (summary order) (rejecting substantive due process challenge to vaccination mandate based on Jacobson).

II. Free Exercise of Religion

Plaintiffs next argue that the temporary exclusion from school of the Phillips and Mendoza-Vaca children during the chicken pox outbreak unconstitutionally burdens their free exercise of religion. Jacobson did not address the free exercise of religion because, at the time it was decided, the Free Exercise Clause of the First Amendment had not yet been held to bind the states. See Cantwell v. Connecticut, 310 U.S. 296, 303 (1940). Therefore, Jacobson does not specifically control Phillips's and Mendoza-Vaca's free exercise claim. The Supreme Court has stated in persuasive dictum, however, that a parent "cannot claim freedom from compulsory vaccination for the child more than for himself on religious grounds. The right to practice religion freely does not include liberty to expose the community or the child to communicable disease or the latter to ill health or death." Prince v. Massachusetts, 321 U.S. 158, 166-67 (1944). That dictum is consonant with the Court's and our precedents holding that "a law that is neutral and of general applicability need not be justified by a compelling governmental interest even if the law has the incidental effect of burdening a particular religious practice." Church of the Lukumi Babalu Aye, Inc. v. City of Hialeah, 508 U.S. 520, 531 (1993); accord, Leebaert v. Harrington, 332 F.3d 134, 143-44 (2d Cir. 2003) (holding that parental claims of free exercise of religion are governed by rational basis test). Accordingly, we agree with the Fourth Circuit, following the reasoning of Jacobson and Prince, that mandatory vaccination as a condition for admission to school does not violate the Free Exercise Clause. See Workman v. Mingo County Bd. of Educ., 419 F. App'x 348, 353-54 (4th Cir. 2011) (unpublished).

New York could constitutionally require that all children be vaccinated in order to attend public school. New York law goes beyond what the Constitution requires by allowing an exemption for parents with genuine and sincere religious beliefs. Because the State could bar Phillips's and Mendoza-Vaca's children from school altogether, a fortiori, the State's more limited exclusion during an outbreak of a vaccine-preventable disease is clearly constitutional.

III. Equal Protection

Plaintiffs argue that the mandatory vaccination provision violates their rights under the Equal Protection Clause. To the extent that plaintiffs are claiming discrimination against Catholics, that argument plainly fails because Phillips and Mendoza-Vaca are both Catholic and received religious exemptions.

Plaintiffs alternatively argue that Check was treated differently than her similarly-situated co-plaintiffs. But, as discussed above, plaintiffs failed to challenge the district court's finding that Check's views on vaccines were not based on sincere religious beliefs. Plaintiffs have put nothing in the record to suggest that Phillips's and Mendoza-Vaca's religious beliefs are similar to Check's. Plaintiffs therefore fail adequately to allege an equal protection violation.

IV. Ninth Amendment

Plaintiffs finally seek succor in the Ninth Amendment. But, we have held, "[t]he Ninth Amendment is not an independent source of individual rights." Jenkins v. C.I.R., 483 F.3d 90, 92 (2d Cir. 2007). Because plaintiffs fail plausibly to allege a violation of any other constitutional right, their effort to recast their unsuccessful claims as a violation of the Ninth Amendment also fails. See id. At 93.

V. Claims in Plaintiffs' Motion for Reconsideration

Plaintiffs also raise numerous arguments on appeal based on a deposition of DOE official Julia Sykes and other documents that they obtained in discovery. Those arguments were raised for the first time in plaintiffs' motion for reconsideration and therefore were not properly presented to the district court. Accordingly, they are waived. See Sompo Japan Ins. Co. of Am. v. Norfolk S. Ry. Co., 762 F.3d 165, 188 (2d Cir. 2014) (declining to consider arguments raised for the first time in motion for reconsideration where no reason exists to excuse untimeliness).

CONCLUSION

For the foregoing reasons, the order of the district court is

AFFIRMED.

1. In 110 years, has there been any change in the Supreme Court's position on the laws concerning vaccination exemption? Why?

"PARENTS FOUND GUILTY IN SON'S MENINGITIS DEATH ARE BEING RIGHTLY PUNISHED," BY ANDRÉ PICARD, FROM *THE GLOBE AND MAIL*, APRIL 29, 2016

David and Collet Stephan failed to seek medical care for their 19-month-old son, Ezekiel, in a timely fashion and he died. For that, they were found guilty of failing to provide the necessities of life, and rightly so.

The parents' failings were egregious: Their toddler became increasingly ill to the point where he was lethargic and stiff as a board; they were told by a nurse that the boy was likely suffering from meningitis, a life-threatening condition; and urged by a naturopath to bring the child to a doctor, but they did not, opting instead for naturopathic "treatments" such as an echinacea tincture. They didn't call 911 until Ezekiel stopped breathing and, by the time he was airlifted to hospital, it was too late to save him.

Despite the conviction, they remain unrepentant, painting themselves as persecuted and warning that the parenting police are out to get us all.

Hardly.

The message in the conviction is consistent with what our laws and courts have said over decades in cases with similar philosophical underpinnings – parents who refuse blood transfusion, vaccination, cancer treatment and other demonstrably beneficial medical treatments for their children in favour of prayer or other nonsense: As an adult, you can have beliefs, religious or otherwise, and you can raise your children according to those beliefs, no matter how wacky, but that does not obviate the obligation to provide the necessities of life. When a child's health and well-being are compromised, the rules change, because a guardian has responsibilities as well as rights.

Put another way, children cannot give consent to the denial of treatment, so they are entitled to the accepted standard of care. In Ezekiel's case, he should have been treated with intravenous fluids, pain relief and antibiotics; what he got instead was chili pepper smoothies and fluids from an eye-dropper. And that is criminal. (And to those who wonder if conventional medicine could have saved the boy, the answer is: We'll never know. The parents' failure was not giving him a fighting chance.)

This case raises many difficult questions for regulators and policy-makers.

Is naturopathy – a belief system that has no scientific basis – a legitimate health profession? After all, in Alberta and a number of other provinces, it is recognized as such, allowing naturopaths to self-regulate.

Should Health Canada give legitimacy to the naturopathic and homeopathic concoctions such as those that were used by approving and regulating "natural health products"? Because, again, there is no scientific evidence of their benefit.

But the most important question of all is: Why have Canadians embraced so-called complementary and alternative treatments so broadly and enthusiastically?

Much of what is espoused – take care of yourself, be attuned to your body, think about where your food comes from, etc. – is quite sensible and healthy.

But there is also a lot of pseudoscientific nonsense out there, from homeopathy (with its ridiculous core belief that diluting medicine in water makes it stronger) to the rejection of vaccines as poison – much of it promoted by "alternative" practitioners such as naturopaths and chiropractors, and high-profile crackpots like Dr. Mercola – that too many people embrace uncritically.

What people seem to be yearning for is some control over their health, and some hands-on care, things that are all-too-often unavailable in the rushed, paternalistic mainstream health system. They also are skeptical

– and not totally without reason – of some of the machinations of pharmaceutical companies.

Pseudoscience is comforting: It's easy to embrace, promising magic and definitive answers, not all messy and rife with unanswered questions like real science. Add to this a lot of flowery language about "natural," "holistic" and "drug-free" treatments, and a dash of scientific illiteracy, and you have a potent cocktail that can, on occasion, have horrible consequences.

Beyond the death of Ezekiel, however, the real tragedy is that there are a lot of David and Collet Stephans out there – parents who are well-meaning but, nonetheless, harming their children.

The answer is not to prosecute and jail them all, it is to educate them, and to above all else, encourage them to be at least as doubtful and skeptical about "alternative" treatments as they are mainstream ones.

In this case, nobody has argued that the parents harmed their child deliberately but, as the prosecutor said at the end of the trial: "Sometimes love just isn't enough."

Sometimes – no, all the time – making the right choices to ensure a child's well-being has to supersede all other considerations.

1. Do you think the parents of Ezekiel should be charged for their son's death?
2. What resources are available for people who need expert help in making health care decisions?

When you fail to do so, like Ezekiel's parents, you have to take your medicine.

"ITALIAN MMR AUTISM DECISION OVERTURNED," BY DORIT RUBINSTEIN REISS, FROM THE SKEPTICAL RAPTOR, APRIL 2, 2016

This article reviews a recent ruling from an Italian Court of appeals that overturns a widely ridiculed decision by a Provincial Court in 2012 that claimed that the MMR vaccine (for measles, mumps, and rubella) causes autism. Apparently, that court rejected all other science, and only accepted the fraudulent work of Mr Andy Wakefield to validate the claims about the vaccine and autism. The Italian MMR autism decision has started to return as a zombie trope, probably as a result of the kerfuffle about the anti-vaccine propaganda movie, Vaxxed.

In June 2012, a provincial court in Rimini, Italy granted compensation to the family of a child named Valentino Bocca. The family alleged that the MMR vaccine Valentino received as part of his childhood immunizations caused his autism, and the court compensated them on that theory. The lower court's decision was never on very firm grounds: it depended in part on testimony of an expert witness who relied, in turn, on Andrew Wakefield's debunked study. Unfortunately, this Italian MMR autism decision has been used by anti-vaccine activists as part of their claims that vaccines cause autism.

THE ITALIAN MMR AUTISM COURT DECISION

On February 13, 2015, a Court of Appeals in Bologna overturned the decision – a decision that apparently lead to a decline in MMR immunization rates in Romagna, an historical district of Italy.

The Court of Appeal accepted the appeal filed by the Ministry of Health (ministero della Sanità). The expert appointed by the court of appeal highlighted that there is no scientific evidence supporting an MMR autism link. The expert highlighted that the lower court expert was wrong to rely on the study by Andrew Wakefield, a study debunked and rejected by the scientific community.

The expert also highlighted that while there is some temporal link between Valentino's MMR vaccine and autism, in the sense that the diagnosis of autism followed the vaccine, the temporal connection was not strong and does not itself support a causal connection.

The expert, Dr. Lodi, stated that "In the medical history of the child there is not an objective temporal correlation between the gradual emergence of autistic disorders and the MMR vaccine, there is only the fact that the two events occur one before the other, but as shown, this is not sufficient to relate the two events."

The Bocca's lawyer, Luca Ventaloro, claimed that he will appeal to the Supreme Court of Cassation (Corte Suprema di Cassazione), the highest court in Italy. He based his intention to appeal on a claim that the expert ignored the latest studies, and highlighted that he is in touch with Andrew Wakefield. There are three problems with that claim:

A. As far as I know, there are no credible studies, recent or otherwise, that actually support a link between vaccines and autism. There are some fatally flawed published studies, for example, Dr Hooker's retracted study, or Dr Theresa Deisher's problematic work [...]

B. There are several recent large scale reviews that highlight the lack of such a link [...]

C. Andrew Wakefield is not a reliable source on anything related to vaccines, given his history. He has a history of serious ethical violations, of research fraud, of misrepresenting evidence in his self-justificatory book (pdf), Callous Disregard, and in his complaint to the Office of Research Integrity in the CDC, in connection with the so-called #CDCwhistleblower manufactroversy.

In short, the lawyer's claims have no basis.

Furthermore, appeals to the Court of Cassation cannot be taken on matters of fact, only on matters of law. The claim of ignoring studies seems like a matter of fact–that is, the court got its fact wrong. This should not, on its face, be good grounds for appeal.

While Ventaloro, attorney for the plaintiffs, said he's optimistic, I expect – and hope – that his optimism, based on such an unfounded set of facts and weak legal basis is misplaced, and that the Court of Cassation will do the right thing, follow the science and uphold the Court of Appeal's decision. Science shows there is no link between vaccines and autism. On scientific questions, courts should follow the science.

1. Why was the original decision regarding a purported vaccine injury overturned by Italy's Court of Appeals?

"NM V. HEBREW ACADEMY LONG BEACH BEACH ET AL," UNITED STATES DISTRICT COURT EASTERN DISTRICT OF NEW YORK, DECIDED JANUARY 9, 2016

NM, Individually and on Behalf of EK and LK,
Minors,
Plaintiffs,

-against-

HEBREW ACADEMY LONG BEACH, LANCE HIRT, Individually and in his Official Capacity as President of Hebrew Academy Long Beach, RICHARD HAGLER, Individually and in his Official Capacity as Executive Director of Hebrew Academy Long Beach, DOVID PLOTKIN, Individually and in his Official Capacity as Principal of Hebrew Academy Long Beach, MARY ELLEN ELIA, in her Official Capacity as Commissioner, New York State Education Department, DR. HOWARD M. ZUCKER, MD, JD, in his Official Capacity as Commissioner, New York State Department of Health,

Defendants

[...]

SPATT, DISTRICT JUDGE:

This case involves a constitutional challenge to New York's requirement that school-aged children be vaccinated against certain communicable diseases in order to attend classes.

The Plaintiff, identified for purposes of this action as NM, commenced this action on behalf of herself and her two minor children, identified as EK and LK (together, the "Minors," and collectively with NM, the "Plaintiffs"), against the Hebrew Academy of Long Beach ("HALB"), its President Lance Hirt ("Hirt"), its Executive Director Richard Hagler ("Hagler"), its Principal Dovid Plotkin ("Plotkin," together with HALB, Hirt, and Hagler, the "School Defendants"), as well as New York State's Commissioner of Education Mary Ellen Elia ("Elia"), and New York State's Commissioner of Health Howard M. Zucker, M.D., J.D. ("Dr. Zucker," together with Elia, the "State Defendants").

The complaint alleges violations of federal and state laws, including causes of action based on Section 2164 of the New York Public Health Law; Section 296 of the New York Human Rights Law; the First, Ninth, and Fourteenth Amendments to the United States Constitution; and Article 1 of the New York State Constitution.

Presently before the Court is a motion by the Plaintiffs, brought on by Order to Show Cause, seeking a preliminary injunction directing the School Defendants to permit the Minors to attend HALB during the pendency of this lawsuit without receiving the required vaccinations.

I. BACKGROUND

A. OVERVIEW OF THE RELEVANT STATUTORY PROVISIONS

Before delving into the specific facts of this case, the Court finds that it will be helpful to provide an overview of the legal framework governing the intersection of religious beliefs and state-mandated vaccinations.

Section 2164 of the New York Public Health Law (the "PHL") imposes a baseline requirement that school-aged children be immunized against certain enumerated diseases. In relevant part, the statute provides as follows:

> No principal, teacher, owner or person in charge of a school shall permit any child to be admitted to such school, or to attend such school, in excess of fourteen days, without the [appropriate certificate by an administering physician] or some other acceptable evidence of the child's immunization against poliomyelitis, mumps, measles, diphtheria, rubella, varicella, hepatitis B, pertussis, tetanus, and, where applicable, Haemophilus influenza type b (Hib), *meningococcal disease*, and pneumococcal disease . . . PHL § 2164(7)(a).

However, the PHL carves out two express exemptions from this general requirement, namely: (i) a medical exemption for children whose pediatrician certifies that the required immunizations may be detrimental to their health, see PHL § 2164(8); and (ii) a religious exemption. Relevant here, the religious exemption removes from the statute's purview "children whose parent, parents, or guardian hold genuine and sincere religious beliefs which are contrary to" the practice of vaccinating, and, as to them, requires no certificate of immunization as a prerequisite to their attendance at school. See PHL § 2164(9).

With this basic statutory scheme in mind, the Court turns to the relevant facts of this case, which are drawn primarily from the testimony provided during a related evidentiary hearing held on January 4, 2016, together with the affidavits and supporting exhibits submitted in connection with the Plaintiffs' motion.

THE PARTIES

The Defendant HALB is a school system comprised of four individual educational institutions, namely, the Lev Chana Early Childhood Center; HALB Elementary; the SKA High School for Girls; and the DRS High School for Boys. HALB offers a bicultural education in both general and Judaic studies from nursery school through high school, and has a total enrollment of approximately 1,675 students. See Dec. 21, 2015 Affidavit of Richard Hagler ("Hagler Aff."), ¶ 3.

The Plaintiff NM is a graduate of Touro College, where she earned a Bachelor's degree, and Fordham University, where she earned Master's and Doctorate degrees in Psychology. The record is unclear as to whether NM is currently employed. She and her husband, a practicing attorney, have three daughters, ages 11, 8, and 3. The Court notes that the Minors in this case, namely, EK and LK, are the Plaintiff's eldest two children.

NM is a devout Orthodox Jew and has raised her three daughters in the Orthodox Jewish tradition. For reasons that NM alleges are inexorably linked to her faith, she has not vaccinated her children and does not intend to do so.

C. HALB'S METHOD OF EVALUATING REQUESTS FOR RELIGIOUS EXEMPTIONS

From 2010 to 2015, the Minors EK and LK attended HALB. During that time, neither child was vaccinated as required by the terms of the PHL. In 2010 and 2012, NM applied for religious exemptions on behalf of her daughters, which were granted in both instances. See Dec. 4, 2015 Affidavit of the Plaintiff ("Pl. Aff."), ¶¶ 24-25. However, in 2015, HALB reevaluated the children's entitlement to an exemption.

The Plaintiffs contend that this resulted from a new policy instituted by HALB at the suggestion of its Board of Directors, namely, to deny religious exemptions to its students. In this regard, NM asserted that, in May 2015, she received a telephone call from the school nurse, advising her that HALB "was instituting a policy change and would no longer be accepting religious exemptions." Pl. Aff. ¶ 26. Consistent with this assertion, the Plaintiffs submitted an e-mail, dated May 21, 2015, from an unidentified sender, which, in turn, attached a memorandum purportedly issued by the school nurses, namely, Devorah Sokol RN and Wendy Weiss RN. See Compl., Ex. "2." The memo states, in part, that "HALB does not accept any Religious Exemption to Immunization. Only a Medical exemption can excuse a student from a vaccine, beliefs do not." Id.

HALB's President, Lance Hirt, testified that the information circulated by the school nurses was inaccurate and did not reflect any official position of HALB. In this regard, the School Defendants deny that any "new policy" regarding religious exemptions was enacted, or that HALB ever determined to categorically refuse religious exemptions to its students. However, the School Defendants do acknowledge that, in mid-2015, they altered HALB's internal procedures for evaluating requests for religious exemptions, in order to make the process more intensive.

In particular, Hirt testified that, in early 2015, numerous parents had begun contacting the administration in response to reports of a measles outbreak in California. Hirt stated that these concerned parents inquired into HALB's preparedness for such an event, as well as the adequacy of the measures being employed to prevent such an outbreak among their own children. According to Hirt, these events prompted HALB to assess the sufficiency of its procedure for determining which students should be excused from receiving the State-mandated vaccines.

Hirt testified that, upon reflection, HALB found its own enforcement of PHL § 2164 to be below the legal standard. In particular, he stated that the school had not previously conducted any meaningful review of students' applications for religious exemptions, and that the administration had simply "rubber stamped" such requests without conducting due diligence. In this regard, Hirt testified that the Plaintiffs' requests for religious exemptions in 2010 and 2012 were likely approved without any inquiry into the sincerity or genuineness of their alleged religious beliefs against the practice of vaccinating.

Accordingly, in 2015, HALB began "strict enforcement" of the State immunization law by, for example, closely scrutinizing the reasons proffered by parents seeking religious exemptions for their children. See Hagler Aff. ¶ 15 ("We understand it to be the school's duty to assess what the motivation of a family is and whether a religious basis is genuinely held"). To that end - and consistent with Hirt's testimony that the school nurses had inaccurately advised parents of a new school policy against religious exemptions - on July 10, 2015 HALB's Executive Director Richard Hagler sent a letter to the Plaintiffs, stating as follows:

> We write to correct any misunderstandings and to request any documentation and information that may further support your request for a religious exemption from the immunization requirements of New York State law. None of the HALB schools . . . admits or is permitted to admit students who have not been vaccinated in accordance with State law, unless those students fall within the two statutorily provided exemptions.
>
> We require, as we must, the appropriate certificate of immunization for every student as mandated by the above-referenced New York laws [N.Y. Educ. L. § 914; PHL § 2164; 10 N.Y.C.R.R. § 66-1.3].Based on our current understanding of the requirements of State law, we have questions about the genuineness and sincerity of the religious belief basis for your refusal to have your children immunized as required by these statutes.
>
> Accordingly, we request that you either provide us with the state-mandated certification of immunization for each child who seeks to enroll or that you contact the undersigned to arrange for a meeting to discuss your request for an exemption from the statutory and regulatory requirements that we are bound by law to enforce.
>
> Compl., Ex. "5."

In a supporting affidavit, Hagler stated that similar letters were also sent to eight other families who had applied for religious exemptions. See Hagler Aff. ¶¶ 4-5.

D. THE EVALUATION PROCESS

Hagler stated that, of the nine families who received the letter, quoted above, three immediately began the immunization process so that their children could attend HALB; two families withdrew their children from HALB; and four families, including NM and her husband, accepted the school's invitation to meet and discuss their respective requests for an exemption. See Hagler Aff. ¶ 6.

On September 2, 2015, NM and her husband attended a meeting at HALB with Lance Hirt, Richard Hagler, and a pediatrician named Dr. Evan Pockriss, whose own children attend HALB. NM and her husband appeared for this meeting with their counsel, Patricia Finn, Esq.

In a supporting affidavit, NM described the meeting as a "setup." However, she sets forth few factual details to support this characterization. In particular, NM states only that, in her opinion, "[t]here was no genuine interest shown in understanding the religious nature of [her] beliefs." Pl. Aff. ¶ 41. Although she acknowledged being asked by Lance Hirt where in Jewish law there existed a prohibition against vaccinating, she stated that Dr. Pockriss conducted most of the questioning, and that his inquiries were largely "medical[ ] or health related." Id.; Hrg. Tr. at 35 ("Basically the only questions directed to me . . . were directed to me by the pediatrician").

In his opposing affidavit, Richard Hagler disputes NM's account of the meeting and states that she made statements to the HALB representatives which are inconsistent with the position she now takes for purposes of this lawsuit. In particular, according to Hagler, NM acknowledged during the meeting that she had ingested prenatal vitamins during her pregnancies and described herself as the "vitamin queen." Hagler Aff. ¶ 14. Further, according to Hagler, NM indicated that she would administer antibiotics if her daughters required them; that she keeps no sugar in the house; and that her daughters "have 'almost no candy.' " Id. Hagler stated that NM's attorney had remarked at the meeting that laws which exclude unvaccinated children from schools "make no sense; that children vaccinated in the first weeks of school are contagious; and that even dead viruses can turn out to be live." Id. ¶ 17.

Lance Hirt testified consistently with this account. He stated that the interview committee had been "shocked" when NM and her husband appeared for the meeting and "didn't actually talk about sincere religious beliefs with any real focus." Hrg. Tr. 142.

Based on NM's presentation at the meeting, the interviewers unanimously agreed that her reasons for not vaccinating the Minors "were based on perceived health concerns and not sincere religious convictions." Id. ¶ 10. In this regard, Hirt testified that, "[i]n the judgment of [the] committee ... the motivations of the plaintiff were medically oriented and not religious." Hrg. Tr. 134. He testified that NM apparently believed that she "had a better way to protect [the Minors'] health, which was through diet," and that "introducing a foreign substance was not something [she] thought was a good idea from a health perspective." Id. at 140. Thus, according to Hirt, "nothing that [the committee members] heard during those discussions indicated to [them] that it was a religious belief ... that was driving their position on vaccination." Id. Rather, the conclusion drawn by him and the other interviewers was that NM "felt strongly about living a certain healthy lifestyle" and was seeking "a religious perspective that was consistent with" that lifestyle. Id. at 140.

Hagler also disputed NM's assertion that the committee had been uninterested in the sincerity of her religious convictions. In particular, Hagler stated as follows:

> During the meeting with plaintiff and her husband, despite our direct questions for them to explain their religious basis for not vaccinating, they (mostly plaintiff) spent the entire meeting discussing medical concerns and notions of putting a body at risk through the introduction of foreign substances. They told us our way of thinking about vaccines was just wrong and how our science is flawed but said almost nothing about religious beliefs. Ironically, they explained that once they decided not to vaccinate, they then went to consult with Rabbis to make sure they could find a basis in Jewish law to support their decision not to vaccinate. Hagler Aff. ¶ 16.

On September 4, 2015, Hagler sent a letter to NM advising her that HALB had rejected her application for a religious exemption. See id., Ex. "B."

However, the Court notes that, consistent with the School Defendants' contention that HALB does not have a blanket policy against granting religious exemptions to qualified students, there is evidence that, following a similar meeting, the administration had been "convinced of the sincerity and genuineness of the religious objections of one of the families, and, therefore, accepted its application for a religious exemption." Id. ¶ 10. In opposition to the instant motion, the School Defendants submitted a letter that HALB sent to this family advising them of its determination. See Dec. 21, 2015 Affidavit of Philip H. Kalban, Esq. ("Kalban Aff."), Ex. "A."

On September 7, 2015, NM's husband sent a lengthy e-mail to Lance Hirt and Richard Hagler seeking reconsideration of HALB's decision not to grant the Minors a religious exemption. See Hagler Aff., Ex. "C." Although NM testified that her husband was solely responsible for preparing the e-mail, see Hrg. Tr. at 93, the Court nevertheless finds that there is a reasonable basis for imputing the husband's statements regarding their religious beliefs to NM as well.

In this regard, the Court notes that the e-mail is signed on behalf of both NM and her husband. Further, NM testified that she and her husband share substantially the same religious beliefs, and that, following the school's denial of her request for a religious exemption, she did not supply HALB with any additional information clarifying her own beliefs or how, if at all, they differ from those expressed by her husband. See Hrg. Tr. at 62-63 ("Q: [I]s he [your husband] in agreement with you as to your religious beliefs contrary to vaccination? A: Yes, we are in complete agreement"); see also Pl. Aff. ¶ 20 ("My husband shares my religious convictions, and with the approval of our Rabbi, agrees that we must abstain from vaccinating our children").

Further, the September 7, 2015 e-mail from NM's husband outlines a philosophy that is consistent in all material respects with NM's affidavit and hearing testimony, namely, that Jewish law commands its followers to guard their health and refrain from defiling their bodies.

NM asserts that these commandments are inconsistent with the practice of vaccinating, which, by its nature, involves puncturing the skin, introducing a foreign substance into the blood stream, and undermining the Jewish belief that our natural immune system is sufficient to ward off disease.

In this regard, NM's husband states in the e-mail that his and NM's decision not to vaccinate the Minors "stems from a complex interplay of *Halachic* imperatives to guard [their] health, discussions with [their] Posek, Rabbi Chait, and [the Minors'] doctor, Dr. Lawrence Palevsky." He further states that NM "was raised in a home where nutrition and health were synonymous to keeping a kosher home" and that "guarding your own health is actually a *mitzvah*." The e-mail includes numerous citations to religious authorities such as Maimonides for the proposition that "there is a positive obligation in the Torah to guard against bodily injury." The e-mail states that "[i]t is not enough to deal with health issues as they arise; we must take precautions to avoid danger. That is why exercise, a healthy diet and following your doctor's recommendations are obligations that stem from the Torah and are not voluntary." It further states that "[i]t is virtually impossible to separate the area of health from the Torah in any way."

Of prime importance here, NM's husband states that:

> Our pediatrician educated us extensively on the pros and cons of vaccinating our children. ... After discussing this at length with our doctor, we knew that we still had to seek *Da'at Torah* before making this significant decision. We discussed this with Rabbi Chait, who informed us that the

> *Halacha* says to follow our doctor, and that in our case, it would be a *Halachic* problem if we failed to follow our own doctor's recommendations. While our decision not to vaccinate was supported by our doctor and resonated with all of our healthful lifestyle practices, ultimately our decision hinged upon getting a *halachic* stamp of approval from my Rebbi. It is for this reason that we are seeking an exemption only on religious grounds. See Hagler Aff., Ex. "C."

In his opposing affidavit, Hagler stated that the September 7, 2015 e-mail served to reinforce HALB's previous determination that NM's reasons for not vaccinating her children were, in fact, health-based concerns couched as religious doctrine. See Hagler Aff. ¶¶ 21, 26 ("Just because their rabbi told them to 'follow [their] doctor ... ,' [ ] does not transform their health concerns into a religious 'belief'").

Hirt also testified that the September 7, 2015 e-mail did not alter his decision. In particular, he testified that this e-mail made the committee feel "more secure in [its] decision" and left HALB feeling as if it had "made the right decision" following the September 2, 2015 interview. Hrg. Tr. at 146. According to Hirt, the e-mail "made it clear to [the committee] that the [Plaintiffs] had a decision that they made on medical grounds in discussions with their physician, and only then did they go to make sure that it was in compliance, that it was okay under Jewish law not to vaccinate." Id.

On September 7, 2015, Hagler sent a responsive e-mail to NM's husband indicating that there had been no change in HALB's position on the matter, and that, pursuant to New York law, the Minors would be permitted to attend school for two weeks, at which time NM would be required to provide a certificate of immunization. See Compl., Ex. "10."

E. THE EXCLUSION OF THE MINORS FROM HALB

The Minors attended HALB for fourteen days, until October 8, 2015. On that date, Hagler sent a letter to NM advising her that, because the Minors had not been immunized, and had not demonstrated that they had begun the immunization process, they were no longer permitted to attend HALB. See Compl., Ex. "12."

NM testified that she did not take any steps to enroll the students in a different Hebrew school, where a religious exemption might be granted. See Hrg. Tr. at 71-72. Rather, the Minors have been home-schooled since October 8, 2015.

F. THE INSTANT MOTION

On December 10, 2015, the Plaintiffs commenced this action. The next day, December 11, 2015, they moved this Court by Order to Show Cause for preliminary injunctive relief. In support of that request, NM submitted an affidavit setting forth the nature of her allegedly genuine and sincerely-held religious beliefs contrary to vaccinating her children.

In her affidavit, NM asserts that her religious beliefs are rooted in the holy Torah and its commandments, which govern all areas of her life. See Pl. Aff. ¶ 5. In this regard, the Torah commands that "the human body is God's perfect creation ... and its purity and integrity must be maintained." Id. ¶ 8. To that end, "[m]any of God's commandments address the care of the human body via precautions regarding cleanliness and the instruction to keep the body healthy without defilement." Id. ¶ 10. For example, "[t]he Torah specifically rejects the acts of making cuttings in the flesh, imprinting marks, and defilement of the body via impure substances." Id. ¶ 11. Thus, to the extent that "[v]accines inherently contain disease and other impure substances, [ ] their inoculation into the body is a violation of the dictates of [her] religious beliefs." Id. ¶ 13.

According to NM, "Jewish law prohibits the prophylactic use of medical interventions ... for healthy individuals." Id. ¶ 16. Instead, she contends that "prevention ... primarily through nutrition" is "the highest form of healing" and that which most closely comports with the Judaic precept that observant Jews "live in accordance with the order of creation in nature." Id. ¶¶ 15, 17. In this regard, NM stated that she "strive[s] to live as naturally and healthfully as possible" and that her "pursuit of purity pervades [her] whole way of life, including eating habits and methods of combatting illness." Id. ¶ 18.

On December 16, 2015, the Court signed the Order Show Cause and directed the parties to appear for an evidentiary hearing on December 22, 2015. The purpose of the hearing would be to develop the record as it related to one discrete factual issue, namely, whether NM held genuine and sincere religious beliefs contrary to the practice of vaccinating, such that a mandatory injunction should issue during the pendency of this lawsuit. The return date of the Order to Show Cause was subsequently adjourned to January 6, 2016.

G. THE HEARING

All parties appeared by counsel for an evidentiary hearing on January 6, 2016.

At the hearing, at which only NM and Lance Hirt, the President of HALB, testified, NM reiterated her belief that the Torah commands her "to keep the body completely whole and pure without defilement." Hrg. Tr. at 16. In this regard, she referred to Jewish beliefs against making cuttings in the flesh, but did not supply any specific quotations. See, e.g., id. at 43, 73-74. She also reiterated her belief in prioritizing natural remedies over invasive medical treatments, stating that "any disease which can be treated naturally should be treated in a natural way." Id. at 38, 40 ("We follow[ ] the way of the Rambam to follow natural health").

Further, NM testified that Jewish law places an emphasis on preventive medicine, but not prophylactic treatment for healthy individuals. See, e.g., id. at 39 (testifying that "the emphasis is on preventive medicine"); id. at 63 (testifying that prophylactic medicine is "forbidden"). Apparently, according to NM, when it comes to treating illness, there is a preferred halachic method, namely, natural non-invasive means, and a method of last resort, namely, invasive medical practice. Id. (explaining that her interpretation of Jewish law "is all about using food as medicine" and that the famous Hebrew scholar Maimonides "instructs us to always go from a natural to the more invasive").

Of importance, NM does not appear to assert that her religion forbids the practice of vaccinating; only that she feels obligated to first pursue less invasive means of disease prevention. See, e.g., id. at 39-40 ("[W]e were always taught that modern medicine was not to be rejected, of course not, but it was always a method of last resort."). In fact, she specifically testified that the duty of observant Jews to protect themselves from disease "does not preclude" the use of immunizations; it simply "says it is not the preferred method." Id. at 99.

In this regard, NM testified as to her understanding that, once she reached a personal conclusion on the issue of vaccinations, her beliefs took on the force of Jewish law, and the Torah required her to follow her conscience in that regard. See id. at 42 ("The system of Halacha is a personal one ... There are a lot of personal subjective issues. ... What we understand from our consultation with [Rabbis] is that ... once we had come to a conclusion ... these beliefs took on the rule of law and that we were not allowed to act against our conscience"); see also id. at 34 (stating that her personal beliefs are what "really matter[ ]").

It was brought out on cross-examination that, despite her reliance upon Jewish teachings against making cuttings in the flesh, NM has her ears pierced. See id. at 75. It was also brought out that NM has permitted herself to be injected with Novocaine during dental procedures. See id. at 111. Also, the Minors use sunscreen, which NM agreed was "a preventative, to prevent them from getting sunburn which [ ] in later life can cause cancer." Id. at 91. It was also brought out that she ingested prenatal vitamin supplements during her pregnancies because they are "practically required by every doctor." Id. at 89. In this regard, she testified that, in order to guard their health, her family "take[s] a lot of dietary nutritional precautions including keeping sugar out of [their] diet" and following "healthful dietary recommendation[s]." Id. at 90.

Asked "[w]here in Jewish law is there a prohibition against immunization," NM responded that "[t]here is a commandment that says protect your health greatly." Id. at 86-87; see also id. at 38 (noting "that one of the positive commandments in the Torah is to guard your health greatly"). However, she conceded that vaccinations are one method of protecting your health, and that immunizations do, in fact, protect people from disease. Id. at 87, 99. Crucial to this case, NM testified on cross-examination that, when it comes to vaccinations, her objection is based, in part, on "contraindications" and "side effects." Id. at 101.

II. DISCUSSION

By this motion, the Plaintiffs seek preliminary relief in the form of a mandatory injunction, during the pendency of this lawsuit, requiring the School Defendants to: (i) reinstate the Minors' religious exemption; and (ii) admit them to HALB without the State-mandated vaccinations.

A. THE PRELIMINARY INJUNCTION STANDARD

"To obtain a preliminary injunction, plaintiff must show irreparable harm absent injunctive relief, and either a likelihood of success on the merits, or a serious question going to the merits to make them a fair ground for trial, with a balance of hardships tipping decidedly in plaintiff's favor." Louis Vuitton Malletier v. Dooney & Bourke, Inc., 454 F.3d 108 (2d Cir. 2006) (citing Jackson Dairy, Inc. v. H.P. Hood & Sons, Inc., 596 F.2d 70, 72 (2d Cir. 1979) (per curiam)); see Christian Louboutin S.A. v. Yves Saint Laurent America Holding, Inc., 696 F.3d 206, 215 (2d Cir. 2012); Rossini v. Republic of Arg., 453 F. App'x 22, 24 (2d Cir. 2011).

"When the movant seeks a 'mandatory' injunction — that is, as in this case, an injunction that will alter rather than maintain the status quo - she must meet the more rigorous standard of demonstrating a 'clear' or 'substantial' likelihood of success on the merits." Rossini, 453 F. App'x at 24 (citing Citigroup Global Mkts, Inc. v. VCG Special Opportunities Master Fund Ltd., 598 F.3d 30, 35 n.4 (2d Cir. 2010)); see D.D. v. N.Y. City Bd. of Educ., 465 F.3d 503, 510 (2d Cir. 2006) ("A party moving for a mandatory injunction that alters the status quo by commanding a positive act must meet a higher standard . . . That is, '[t]he moving party must make a clear or substantial showing of likelihood of success' on the merits" (quoting Jolly v. Coughlin, 76 F.3d 468, 473 (2d Cir. 1996))).

The Court notes that "the preliminary injunction 'is one of the most drastic tools in the arsenal of judicial remedies.' " Grand River Enter. Six Nations, Ltd. v. Pryor, 481 F.3d 60, 66 (2d Cir 2007) (quoting Hanson Trust PLC v. SCM Corp., 774 F.2d 47, 60 (2d Cir. 1985)); see Mazurek v. Armstrong, 520 U.S. 968, 972, 117 S. Ct. 1865, 138 L. Ed. 2d 162 (1997) (" 'It frequently is observed that a preliminary injunction is an extraordinary and drastic remedy, one that should not be granted unless the movant, by a clear showing, carries the burden of persuasion' " (quoting 11A C. Wright, A. Miller, & M. Kane, Federal Practice and Procedure § 2948, pp. 129-130 (2d ed. 1995))); Ticor Title Ins. Co. v. Cohen, 173 F.3d 63, 68 (2d Cir. 1999) ("An award of an injunction is not something a plaintiff is entitled to as a matter of right, but rather it is an equitable remedy issued by a trial court, within the broad bounds of its discretion, after it weighs the potential benefits and harm to be incurred by the parties from the granting or denying of such relief"). Accordingly, the Court has "wide discretion in determining whether to grant a preliminary injunction." Moore v. Consol. Edison Co., 409 F.3d 506, 510 (2d Cir. 2005).

B. THE FIRST ELEMENT - IRREPARABLE HARM

The first and the most important part of the preliminary injunction standard is whether the Plaintiffs will suffer irreparable harm if an injunction does not issue. See Singas Famous Pizza Brands Corp. v. New York Adver. LLC, 468 F. App'x 43, 45 (2d Cir. 2012) (" 'A showing of irreparable harm is *the single most important* prerequisite for the issuance of a preliminary injunction' " (quoting Faiveley Transp. Malmo AB v. Wabtec Corp., 559 F.3d 110, 118 (2d Cir. 2009)) (emphasis supplied)).

The Court notes that, under circumstances similar to those presented here, school-aged children have been deemed irreparably injured as a result of being excluded from attending classes. See, e.g., Caviezel v. Great Neck Public Sch., 701 F. Supp. 2d 414, 426 (E.D.N.Y. 2010) (Spatt, J.), aff'd, 500 F. App'x 16 (2d Cir. 2012), cert. denied, ___ U.S. ___, 133 S. Ct. 1997, 185 L. Ed. 2d 866 (2013). Thus, under the facts of this case, the exclusion of NM's minor children from HALB is certainly evidence of irreparable harm to them.

However, even assuming that this element of the preliminary injunction standard is established, the Plaintiffs have nevertheless failed to sustain their burden of showing a clear or substantial likelihood of succeeding on the merits of their federal and state claims. Thus, as set forth more fully below, a preliminary injunction is not warranted.

C. THE SECOND ELEMENT - LIKELIHOOD OF SUCCESS ON THE MERITS

As the Plaintiffs acknowledge, similar challenges to school administrators' enforcement of the religious exemption from PHL § 2164 have consistently been rejected by this and other courts, and in the process, have generated a body of controlling authority which is dispositive of the claims at issue here. See, e.g., Caviezel, supra, and, more recently, Phillips v. City of New York, 775 F.3d 538 (2d Cir. 2015), cert. denied, ___ U.S. ___, 136 S. Ct. 104, 193 L. Ed. 2d 37 (2015).

In this regard, the Court finds the facts of this case to be analogous to those in Caviezel. In that case, the plaintiffs sought a preliminary injunction compelling the defendant school district to register their four-year old daughter in a pre-K program without receiving the State-mandated vaccinations. Invoking PHL § 2164(9), the plaintiffs contended that their genuine and sincerely-held religious beliefs forbade them from immunizing their children. More particularly, the mother, a self-identified "pantheist," had testified that she saw vaccines as unnecessary because the form of human beings, as created by God, was already "a perfect creation." Similar to NM, the mother in that case "ma[de] a distinction between taking medications because of a disease, and immunization which is putting disease into the body." In that regard, she testified that her choices were "personal" and that she took Motrin for headaches and gave Motrin and peppermint oil to her children for headaches, fevers, and earaches.

In the Caviezel case, the "church" with which the plaintiff was affiliated, namely, the Church of the Beloved, took no position on the propriety of vaccination and had not instructed the plaintiff that she could not get her daughter immunized for school. In fact, the plaintiff's other children had received vaccinations. At a hearing, it was revealed that the mother also objected to vaccinations because she was unsure whether they are safe or whether they can cause autism.

On those facts, this Court found that the plaintiff had failed to establish a "genuine and sincere religious belief," as required by the relevant statute. In particular, the Court noted that, although it was clear that the family sincerely and genuinely opposed vaccinations for the child at issue, the evidence did not establish that those objections were religious in nature. The Court noted that there was no evidence that the plaintiff's church expressed opposition to vaccinations. Further, the Court noted that "one of the reasons" behind the plaintiffs' objection to vaccinations was that the practice "may not be safe." Acknowledging that "[h]er concern in that regard [wa]s real, and understandable," the Court nevertheless held that "it [wa]s not based on a religious belief," but on reasons of health.

Further, the Court noted that although the mother felt that the body was God's perfect creation, she conceded that she had taken Motrin and essential oils, and had administered them to her daughter, thereby "indicating a selective personal belief - not a religious belief." Thus, having found that the plaintiffs in the Caviezel case failed to establish a genuine and sincerely-held religious belief contrary to vaccinating, the Court found no likelihood of success on their federal and state claims, and denied preliminary injunctive relief.

In the Court's view, the facts in this case warrant the same result. In particular, the Court does not doubt that NM and her husband hold a genuine and sincere belief that they should not vaccinate the Minors. As this Court acknowledged in Caviezel, NM's beliefs in this regard are "real, and understandable." However, careful consideration of the current record suggests that these beliefs were formed with a primary view toward the children's health, and not their religion. In this regard, the record clearly does not support a finding that Orthodox Judaism, even as interpreted by these particular Plaintiffs, forbids the practice.

The evidence shows that the Plaintiffs are devoutly religious. However, the evidence connecting this faith to their objection to vaccinating the Minors is tenuous. Initially, as noted, the Plaintiff concedes that there is no tenet of the Orthodox Jewish religion that prohibits the practice of vaccinating. In fact, the evidence shows that, of the approximately 1,700 Orthodox Jewish students at HALB, only a small minority of families, including NM and her husband, purport to interpret Judaic law as prohibiting the practice.

Further, as was true in Caviezel, there is evidence in this case to indicate that NM holds "a selective personal belief" against the practice of vaccinating, as opposed to "a religious belief." In this regard, NM relies primarily on the Torah's commandment to guard the body against disease. However, NM testified that she applies this rule flexibly; that it is her prerogative to determine the best method of guarding the Minors' bodies against disease; and that the full force of Jewish law should attach to her decisions. Of importance, NM concedes that Jewish law "does not preclude" the use of immunizations, and that vaccines do, in fact, protect the body against disease. See id. at 99. However, in her opinion, immunizations are "not the preferred method," id., and she believes that her lifestyle choices, namely, utilizing nutrition as "the highest form of healing," more closely comport with the principles of "liv[ing] in accordance with the order of creation in nature," see Pl. Aff. ¶¶ 15-17. In the Court's view, these facts indicate selective personal beliefs against the practice of vaccinating, not fundamental religious beliefs.

The selectivity with which NM applies the Torah's commandments is also apparent in other parts of her testimony. For example, she has pierced ears, contradicting her purported belief against making cuttings in the skin. She ingests prenatal vitamins because they are doctor recommended, apparently without regard for whether vaccinations are similarly recommended. She permits Novocaine to be injected into her body by a dentist, undermining her objection to foreign impure substances being inoculated into the body. And, despite testifying that Jewish law forbids prophylactic remedies for healthy individuals, she applies sunblock to her daughters' skin to prevent adverse health effects of sun exposure.

In reaching its conclusion, the Court takes special note of NM's testimony that, when it comes to vaccinations, her objection is based, in part, on "contraindications" and "side effects." This is consistent with the e-mail prepared by her husband seeking reconsideration of HALB's determination, which she has not materially disputed. In that e-mail, the husband states that the family's pediatrician educated them as to "the pros and cons of vaccinating" the Minors, and only then did they consult a Rabbi to obtain "a *halachic* stamp of approval." In the Court's view, this evidence supports the conclusion that the Plaintiffs' concerns are substantially health-based, rather than based on sincere and genuine religious beliefs.

Accordingly, the Court finds that the Plaintiffs have not sustained their burden of establishing that they hold genuine and sincere religious beliefs against the practice of vaccinating. Thus, under the authority of Caviezel and its progeny, the Plaintiffs are not likely to succeed on the merits of their federal and state causes of action. Under these circumstances, a preliminary injunction is unwarranted.

III. CONCLUSION

Based on the foregoing, the Court finds that the Plaintiffs have not shown that they hold genuine and sincere religious beliefs which prohibit vaccinations. Therefore, the Plaintiff's motion for a preliminary injunction is denied in all respects.

The parties are directed to contact United States Magistrate Judge Anne Y. Shields to schedule discovery.

SO ORDERED

1. How strictly does a court define a religious objection to vaccinations?
2. Do you agree with this court's findings?

CHAPTER 4

WHAT ADVOCACY ORGANIZATIONS SAY

There are many advocacy organizations campaigning in favor of vaccination programs, operating with the assistance of government health agencies. Private organizations also promote vaccination programs with increased attention to vaccine safety, and a few organizations campaign against mandatory vaccination in general and certain vaccines in particular. "Antivaccine movements conform to a social dynamic that has to do partly with changes in society, partly with the internal dynamics of the neo-Luddite movement, partly with the very success of vaccines in eliminating or reducing feared diseases," writes Arthur Allen in *Vaccine: The Controversial History of Medicine's Greatest Lifesaver*. "Fear of science, dread of change, mistrust of anonymous corporate and government entities, and a nostalgia for a simpler real or imagined past all fed those movements in the past and help explain their resilience."

"WHAT IS I BOOST IMMUNITY?," BY BRITISH COLUMBIA CENTRE FOR DISEASE CONTROL

I Boost Immunity (IBI) is a Canadian-based online grass-roots immunization advocacy program. Our goal is to educate and empower the people who are pro-vaccination by providing a safe platform to discuss ideas, fact based research, and the latest immunization news.

I Boost Immunity is based on a simple idea: raising local awareness about immunization benefits you and your community. At the same time, we recognize that diseases cross local and national boundaries. It means that vaccinating anyone, anywhere in the world, benefits all of us.

This is why we aim to educate our local communities, while simultaneously helping immunization efforts globally through UNICEF.

WHAT IS OUR MISSION?

Our mission is to foster a sense of belonging, ownership and pride about immunization. There's power in the crowd, especially when it's the silent majority. IBI is a platform based on the idea that speaking up and feeling empowered about your choice to vaccinate is long overdue. It's a platform that encourages conversations between friends, co-workers and families in the 'immunity community' about why vaccination is so important.

WHO MANAGES I BOOST IMMUNITY?

We are managed by the Public Health Association of British Columbia (PHABC) and funded by the BC Ministry of Health.

IBI is owned and operated by the PHABC in partnership with ImmunizeBC – a collaboration between the BC Ministry of Health, BC Centre for Disease Control, Provincial Health Services Authority, regional health authorities, and the BC Pharmacy Association.

HOW DOES I BOOST IMMUNITY WORK?

Here's how:

- Educate yourself about immunization by doing Booster quizzes. For each question you get right, I Boost Immunity will purchase a vaccine in support of UNICEF Canada on your behalf.
- Share evidence-based articles and stories from I Boost Immunity through your social networks. Every time you share, I Boost Immunity will purchase a vaccine in support of UNICEF Canada on your behalf.
- Submit your story about why you care about immunization, and earn more vaccines.

Add a positive voice to the immunization conversation in your community. The more you do, the more vaccines you can earn. It's that simple.

WHO PAYS FOR THE VACCINES?

Currently, the cost of vaccines are being seed funded through the Public Health Association of British Columbia. As the platform expands, I Boost Immunity will be looking for foundation partners and corporate sponsors with an interest in global health, vaccination, science and humanitarian education for children or innovative uses of gamification for social change. If you are an organization with an interest in any of these areas, please contact us!

WHAT VACCINES ARE DONATED TO UNICEF?

I Boost Immunity will purchase tetanus, polio or measles vaccines through UNICEF Canada.

WHAT/WHO IS A "BOOSTER"?

I Boost Immunity relies on crowdsourcing the passion, knowledge and experience of people like you - "Boosters" - who are in the silent majority that believe immunization is a shared community value worth celebrating.

Anyone can be a Booster, from healthcare professionals, stay-at-home parents, retirees, students, farmers, bankers, etc. What Boosters share is a passion about preventing sickness, disability, and death caused by vaccine-preventable diseases.

HOW CAN YOU HELP?

You can help in many ways!

- Complete our quizzes
- Submit a story about why immunization is important to you
- Share our articles on social media, and leave comments
- Encourage your friends and family to also come visit I Boost Immunity

1. Where do you go for information on vaccinations?
2. Do you speak to others about the benefits or side effects of vaccinations? Or is it a topic that doesn't often come up? Why?

EXCERPT FROM *VACCINE EPIDEMIC: HOW CORPORATE GREED, BIASED SCIENCE, AND COERCIVE GOVERNMENT THREATEN OUR HUMAN RIGHTS, OUR HEALTH, AND OUR CHILDREN*, EDITED BY LOUISE KUO HABAKUS AND MARY HOLLAND, FROM SKYHORSE PUBLISHING, 2013

CHAPTER 18: THE VACCINE BUBBLE AND THE PHARMACEUTICAL INDUSTRY

BY MICHAEL BELKIN

Vaccines can cause brain damage. Most people are completely unaware of this, but that is exactly how *The Merck Manual*, the largest-selling medical textbook, defines an adverse reaction to a vaccine:

> Encephalitis is inflammation of the brain that occurs when a virus directly infects the brain or

> when a virus or something else triggers inflammation ... Encephalitis can occur in the following ways: A virus directly infects the brain. A virus that caused an infection in the past becomes reactivated and directly damages the brain. *A virus or vaccine triggers a reaction that makes the immune system attack brain tissue (an autoimmune reaction)* [emphasis added].[1]

An adverse reaction that causes brain damage (encephalitis) is the same thing as a complication from an infectious disease. Any pediatrician, doctor, or state or federal public-health official who tells you that vaccines are completely safe, that adverse reactions to vaccines don't exist, or that vaccine-induced injuries are so rare that they virtually never occur is either ignorant or is committing scientific fraud. Is it worse to have your child vaccinated by a doctor who does not know the possible adverse reactions, or to be lied to by a doctor or government bureaucrat who does know the terrible damage vaccines can cause?

This is no trivial matter. Every day, uninformed physicians administer vaccines to vast numbers of children and adults with little thought about the possibility of adverse reactions. When an adverse reaction occurs—in the form of brain inflammation, convulsions, or another injury—the typical first step is to blame someone else. Doctors and the government accuse parents of child abuse (i.e., shaken baby syndrome) or bad luck (i.e., defective genes) and accuse teenagers of bad behavior (i.e., using illicit drugs). Medical professionals do not step up and ask whether they hold any responsibility for causing an adverse reaction to a vaccine.

The Merck Manual further defines the symptoms of encephalitis: "Symptoms of encephalitis include fever, headache, personality changes or confusion, seizures, paralysis or numbness, sleepiness that can progress to coma and death." Many tens of thousands of parents whose children were diagnosed with autism spectrum disorder reported that their kids were progressing normally until they received one or many vaccines, after which they had fevers, headaches, seizures, personality changes, and were never the same again. The symptoms reported by parents are the same symptoms of encephalitis that are defined in *The Merck Manual*. Health authorities in charge of defending and expanding universal immunization programs label these same symptoms "a coincidence."[2]

When my fve-week-old daughter, Lyla, died hours after receiving her hepatitis B vaccine, the New York medical examiner was more concerned about examining our apartment for evidence of child abuse than about the possibility that a vaccine caused her death. The medical examiner initially told us, our pediatrician, and an investigating pathologist that Lyla'sbrain was so swollen that it led to her death. After consulting with Merck (the manufacturer of Lylas hepatitis B vaccine), the medical examiner left me, a devastated father who just lost his precious fistborn child to an avoidable vaccine-induced death, with these parting words: "We've changed our minds; her brain was not swollen. Vaccines do a lot of good things for people, Mr. Belkin." Former *New York Times* journalist Melody Petersen, who covered the pharmaceutical industry in her book *Our Daily Meds*, reports that doctors who fill out death certificates are instructed to call a "therapeutic misadventure" a natural death.[3]

Vaccine-caused diseases and deaths are an unacknowledged epidemic. The Centers for Disease Control and Prevention (CDC), state public health departments, Bill Gates, and doctors incessantly repeat the mantra calling for more vaccines to eliminate "vaccine-preventable disease." However, my daughter experienced the opposite effect—the prophylactic treatment that was supposed to prevent a disease instead caused severe harm. The medical term for this outcome is iatrogenesis, the "inadvertent and preventable induction of disease or complications by the medical treatment or procedures of a physician or surgeon."[4] To put this in real world terms, you walk in to a doctor's office in perfect health and you walk out with a lifelong neurolocial disability, or you even die, from prescribed vaccines. That is what happened to my daughter. Through immunization programs, modern medicine is creating the epidemic of neurological damage that it takes credit for preventing.

1. Does this personal account of this potential vaccine injury change your mind about vaccines? Why or why not?

"IS HPV VACCINE SAFETY AN ILLUSION MAINTAINED BY SUPPRESSION OF SCIENCE?" BY NORMA ERICSON, FOR *SANEVAX*, JANUARY 15, 2016

Breaking news: On January 14, 2016, Dr. Sin Hang Lee sent an open letter of complaint to the Director General of the World Health Organization, Dr. Margaret Chan, charging members of GACVS [the Global Advisory Committee on Vaccine Safety], the CDC, the Japanese Ministry of Health, Labor and Welfare, and others with manipulation of data and suppression of science in order to maintain the illusion of HPV vaccine safety in the face of valid contradictory evidence.

According to Dr. Lee's letter, a series of emails recently uncovered via a Freedom of Information request submitted in New Zealand revealed evidence that Dr. Robert Pless, chairperson of the Global Advisory Committee on Vaccine Safety (GACVS), Dr. Nabae Koji of the Ministry of Health of Japan, Dr. Melinda Wharton of the CDC, Dr. Helen Petousis-Harris of Auckland University, New Zealand, and others (including WHO officials) may have been actively involved in a scheme to deliberately mislead the Japanese Expert Inquiry on human papillomavirus (HPV) vaccine safety before, during and after the February 26, 2014 public hearing in Tokyo.

The complaint letter states that the emails provided clearly demonstrate this group of WHO officials and government employees charged with the responsibility of advising the expert committee from the Japanese government on HPV vaccination safety knew before the February 26, 2014 Tokyo public hearing that one of their own experts showed scientific evidence that HPV vaccination does increase cytokines, including tumor necrosis factor (TNF), particularly at the injection site compared to other vaccines. Yet, they chose to suppress this information at the public hearing.

Of course, this piece of scientific data which was known to all members of the group is also missing from the GACVS Statement on the safety of HPV vaccination issued on March 12, 2014. Unfortunately for medical consumers, this is the same GACVS statement currently being used to assure health officials, political decision makers and medical professionals around the world there is nothing to worry about when it comes to the safety of HPV vaccines.

- Dr. Lee concluded his letter of complaint by clearly stating that there is at least one known mechanism of action explaining why serious adverse reactions occur more often in people injected with HPV vaccines than other vaccines, and why certain predisposed individuals may suffer a sudden unexplained death as a result. It appears this is part of the information the 'experts' deemed necessary to suppress.

Dr. Lee states:

Those whose names appear in my complaint and any who blindly dismiss valid safety concerns in order to continue promoting HPV vaccinations should be held accountable for their actions. There is no excuse for intentionally ignoring scientific evidence. There is no excuse for misleading global vaccination policy makers at the expense of public health interests. There is no excuse for such a blatant violation of the public trust.

1. What does it mean when doctors disagree about vaccine science? Does this mean that all vaccine science is untrustworthy?

EXCERPT FROM "HPV VACCINE DEBATE IN SOUTH AFRICA," BY NORMA ERICKSON, FROM *SANEVAX*, JANUARY 6, 2016

9 August 2015, a citizen of South Africa (we'll call her Sarah) sent the following questions about HPV vaccines to CANSA, the Cancer Association of South Africa. Sarah had no idea her questions would lead to a full-blown scientific debate.

Could you please let me know why CANSA is supporting the use of the HPV vaccines when these are now proven to be deadly? Several hundred young women have died because of this

> *vaccine and thousands more are permanently disabled or battling with chronic health-problems. This vaccine has NEVER been proven to prevent cervical cancer. Many countries have banned these vaccines because they are not just useless, they are dangerous – why is South Africa using them? And why does your web page not list the potential side effects?*

Sarah received a reply on August 13th referring her to Professor Michael Herbst, a clinical expert who would answer her questions. Professor Herbst sent Sarah copies of 5 abstracts from peer-reviewed scientific journal articles which stated the following. [...]

- ...trials have proven its (HPV vaccine) efficacy in preventing cervical intraepithelial neoplasia (CIN) beyond doubt and its effectiveness in preventing cervical cancer though presumptive is reasonably certain as per mathematical modelling. It also prevents other HPV related anogenital and oropharyngeal malignancies in both sexes.
- The HPVs vaccine prevents infection with certain species of HPVs associated with the development of cervical cancer, genital warts, and some less common cancers.
- The cost-effectiveness of human papillomavirus (HPV) 16/18 vaccination of 12 year-old girls was calculated for 28 countries, under the assumption that vaccination prevents 70% of all cervical cancer cases and that cervical cancer and all-cause mortality rates are stable without vaccination. At three-dose vaccination costs of I$ 100 per vaccinated girl (currency 2005

international dollars), HPV16/18 vaccination was very cost-effective in 25 out of 28 countries...

- Human papillomavirus (HPV) infection is a central and necessary, although not sufficient, cause of cervical cancer. Besides HPV, the additional multiple risk factors related with the onset of cervical cancer are early-age sexual activities; high number of sexual partners, which is the most salient risk factor; suppression and alteration of the immune status; long-term use of oral contraceptives; and other hormonal influences.
- Our analysis (of 24 Hispanic mothers/28 daughters) found several themes that affect whether Hispanic girls get the HPV vaccine: gaps in knowledge; fears and concerns about the vaccine; sociocultural communication practices; and decision-making about HPV vaccination. Both mothers and girls had limited knowledge about cervical cancer, HPV, and the vaccine.

As you can clearly see, Professor Herbst's reply did not address any of the questions Sarah had asked. Undaunted, she replied to him on August 16th as follows (excerpts):

> Dear Prof Herbst
>
> Thank you for the document containing various abstracts to papers on the subject of HPV. With all due respect, these are obviously of zero value in terms of answering the questions that I put to CANSA.
>
> My specific questions are:

Why is CANSA supporting the use of the HPV vaccines when these are now proven to be deadly and when they have NEVER been proven to prevent cervical cancer? Both India and Japan have stopped giving this vaccine because of the severe side effects – why is South Africa ignoring the glut of data that shows this vaccine is dangerous? (Followed by multiple reference documents)

What we do need to do is look at the reported adverse events and to ask the pertinent questions regarding the safety of this vaccine. No manufacturer is going to admit (unless forced to by a court of law) that their product is either defective or deadly.

If anyone purports to be a caring physician and who wishes to help the community defend itself against deadly diseases, then surely that person needs to look at both sides of the argument? It is completely unacceptable simply to point towards the manufacturer and trust that their data is 100% accurate. Attached is a document that lists many of the criminal activities of (and fines handed down to) various pharmaceutical companies. These are the reasons why a good proportion of the general public does not trust the pharmaceutical industry.

Patients have a right to know the risks and benefits of any medical treatment offered to them. Attached is a document that gives pertinent information for South Africans, including the issue of informed consent. This information should be made known to the patient BEFORE the administration of this vaccine.

> I therefore respectfully ask that you go through the above information and then kindly answer my questions.

Several emails were exchanged over the next few days, culminating with this request to Sarah from Professor Herbst on August 20th:

> Please forward to CANSA any scientific evidence (unbiased peer-reviewed research) / scientific reference that supports and proves that:
>
> HPV vaccines are deadly
>
> - That several hundred women have died as a direct result of the vaccine (please reference country / countries where women have died & number of women who have died)
> - That the HPV vaccine was directly responsible for the disability / disabilities that are claimed to result from HPV vaccine (include disability type, numbers affected and country)
> - That there is a direct link between HPV vaccine and the chronic health problems you refer to (specific chronic conditions, numbers affected and country) Please forward scientific information regarding the banning of HPV vaccine by different countries together with the scientific grounds on which the vaccine was banned – please also identify the countries by name.

> Find attached a few abstracts of peer-reviewed scientific research which categorically state that HPV vaccine prevents cervical cancer and Google 'PubMed' and then the key words "HPV vaccine Cervical Cancer Prevention" and read further scientific evidence supporting this.

Professor Herbst had been very careful in the wording of his request to Sarah. He knew, or should have known, exactly how difficult it would be to prove HPV vaccines have been the direct cause of any permanent disability or death. Sarah was not intimidated. She took on the challenge.

By 13 September 2015, she sent Professor Herbst an email with a 105-page document, complete with references from around the world to back up her personal concerns regarding HPV vaccines and vaccination programs. [...]

As of November 15th Sarah had not received a reply from anyone at CANSA, so she sent a short email reminding them she was not going away. She stated she intended to pursue the matter and go public with the truth about how she had been treated with regard to the HPV vaccine matter.

17th November, Professor Herbst had CANSA's Information Coordinator send Sarah a copy of the CANSA's Fact Sheet on Human Papillomavirus Infection and Cancer. [...]

6th December, Sarah responded to the latest email stating:

Thank you for the email from Radiah but there was no response from you to my questions. Attached was a document that is merely standard information and which contains gross inaccuracies such as:-

"Are the HPV vaccines safe and effective? Both the vaccines as said to be safe and effective. Both vaccines were tested in thousands of people around the world. These studies showed no serious side effects. Common, mild side effects included pain where the shot was given, fever, headache, and nausea. As with all vaccines, CDC and FDA continue to monitor the safety of these vaccines very carefully."

Clearly the above is not a response from you but is just a regurgitation from the manufacturer.

Where is the scientific evidence behind "both the vaccines are said to be safe and effective"? Who said they are "safe and effective"? Where is the evidence to back up this claim?

Approximately two and a half hours later, Professor Herbst responds with the following message:

Dear Ms XXX

March 12, 2014 Global Advisory Committee on Vaccine Safety Statement on the continued safety of HPV vaccination as with all new vaccines, the

Global Advisory Committee on Vaccine Safety has been reviewing the safety of HPV vaccines since they were first licensed in 2006. The World Health Organization (WHO) recommends the introduction of HPV vaccination into national immunization programmes where prevention of cervical cancer is a public health priority and the introduction is programmatically feasible [1]. While early detection of pre- and cancerous cells through screening programs has helped decrease incidence rates of cervical cancer in women aged 25-45 in the UK, for example [2], that decrease has plateaued in the past decade. While safety concerns about HPV vaccines have been raised, these have systematically been investigated: to date, the GACVS has not found any safety issue that would alter any of the current recommendations for the use of the vaccine.

The purpose of this update is to summarize the work of GACVS over the past six years in reviewing the safety of HPV vaccines. It is important to highlight and reiterate this work because a number of national immunization programs have been facing real and potential public losses of confidence in their programs as a result of increased negative publicity, even from safety issues that have been addressed.

To date, the GAVCS has reviewed evidence related to syncope, anaphylaxis, venous thromboembolism, adverse pregnancy outcomes, Guillain Barre Syndrome, and stroke [3]. It also examined concerns around the aluminium adjuvant used in HPV vaccines, with considerations around the toxicology of aluminium adjuvants and studies by investigators claiming that aluminium in the quantities used in vaccines are associated with adverse health outcomes[4]. Finally the Committee also reviewed the question of autoimmune disease, specifically around multiple sclerosis (MS), cerebral vasculitis, and an evolving concern over cases of complex regional pain syndrome (CRPS) and/or other chronic pain conditions following vaccination that have surfaced.

With respect to aluminium, the GACVS has had occasion to review the safety of the adjuvant on several occasions, beginning in 1999. At that time, deltoid muscle biopsies performed in France on a number of patients with a variety of complaints revealed in a small number the presence of a minute inflammatory focus of macrophages with associated necrosis. These localized lesions, called macrophagic myofasciitis (MMF), have been shown to contain aluminium salts [5, 6]. Since the location of the lesions in the deltoid muscle coincides with the usual site of injection for vaccines, these microscopic lesions may appear to be related to immunization. The investigators from the "Groupe d'études et de recherche sur les maladies musculaires acquises et dysimmunitaires" (GERMAAD) have suggested that vaccination and localized MMF lesions might be associated with a multi-system disorder. The GACVS has reviewed evidence regarding MMF on several occasions since that time and continues to reaffirm that, while MMF is clearly linked to a vaccination "tattoo" among some patients who have received an aluminium containing vaccine, the associated systemic symptoms related to that finding have never been scientifically proven. Statements about MMF were published in 1999, 2002 and 2004 [4]. While there have never been any published reports of MMF in recipients of HPV vaccines, there is no plausible reason to suspect that any reports of MMF would be associated with systemic symptoms following aluminium containing HPV vaccines any more than the finding of the histological lesion of MMF following hepatitis B vaccine and clinical symptoms.

In 2012, the GACVS reviewed two studies claiming an association between aluminium in vaccines and autism spectrum disorder [7, 8]. It found serious flaws in the two studies that limited their value even for hypothesis generation. In December 2013, the GACVS reviewed evidence related to HPV vaccine and autoimmune disease, specifically multiple sclerosis [3]. While there remain case reports in the literature, multiple epidemiologic studies have not demonstrated any increased risk of autoimmune diseases, including MS, in studies, some of which have included girls who have received HPV vaccine compared to those who had not [9, 10, 11, 12].

Several papers have also been published pertaining to the finding of HPV L1 gene DNA fragments in clinical specimens following HPV vaccination [13, 14]. These papers claimed an association with clinical events of an inflammatory nature, including cerebral vasculitis. While the GACVS has not formally reviewed this work, both the finding of DNA fragments in the HPV vaccine and their postulated relationship to clinical symptoms, have been reviewed by panels of experts. First, the presence of HPV DNA fragments has been addressed by vaccine regulatory authorities who have clearly outlined it as an expected finding given the manufacturing process, and not a safety concern [15]. Second, the case reports [13] of adverse events hypothesized to represent a causal association between the HPV L1 gene DNA fragments and death were flawed in both clinical and laboratory methodology [16]. The paper described 2 fatal cases of sudden death in young women following HPV vaccine, one after 10 days and one after 6 months, with no autopsy findings to support death as result of cerebral vasculitis or an inflammatory syndrome. Thus the hypotheses raised in these papers are not supported by what is understood about the residual DNA fragments left over following vaccine production [17]: given the extremely small quantities of residual HPV DNA in the vaccine, and no evidence of inflammation on autopsy, ascribing a diagnosis of cerebral vasculitis and suggesting it may have caused death is unfounded.

In June 2013, the GACVS reviewed the concerns arising in Japan in regard to reports described as CRPS in a few cases, and other chronic pain conditions following HPV vaccine. At the time, GACVS found no evidence to suggest a causal link with the HPV vaccine, and recommended careful documentation of each case and definition of diagnostic criteria to guide management and causality assessment. The Committee has meanwhile continued to monitor the HPV vaccine and considered further issues during their meeting in December 2013 [3]. In Japan, an expert advisory committee has continued to meet and review the situation but has not yet reached a conclusion. It is acknowledged that the HPV vaccine may be a more painful injection, leading to frequent complaints of pain, which, in some settings, may trigger additional non-specific complaints [18, 19]. As to Complex Regional Pain Syndrome, this entity has been described following various forms of trauma, including injury, surgical procedures and injections. It is therefore plausible that CRPS could develop following the injection of any vaccine (however, such cases have been very rarely described in the literature [20]).In summary, the GACVS continues to closely monitor the safety of HPV vaccines and, based on a careful examination of the available evidence, continues to affirm that its benefit-risk profile remains favorable. The Committee is concerned, however, by the claims of harm that are being raised on the basis of anecdotal observations and reports in the absence of biological or epidemiological substantiation. While the reporting of adverse events following immunization by the public and health care providers should be encouraged and remains the cornerstone of safety surveillance, their interpretation requires due diligence and great care. As stated before, allegations of harm from vaccination based on weak evidence can lead to real harm when, as a result, safe and effective vaccines cease to be used. To date, there is no scientific evidence that aluminium-containing vaccines cause harm, that the presence of aluminium at the injection site (the MMF "tattoo") is related to any autoimmune syndrome, and that HPV DNA fragments are responsible for inflammation, cerebral vasculitis or other immune-mediated phenomena.

Prof Michael C Herbst
Health Specialist
[D Litt et Phil (Health Studies); D N Ed; M Art et Scien; B A Cur; Dip Occupational Health]
Cancer Association of South Africa – Head Office

Address: 26 Concorde Road West, Bedfordview, 2008
Postal: PO Box 2121, Bedfordview, 2008

December 7th, excerpts from Sarah's response:

It greatly concerns me that CANSA appears to have no thoughts of its own and instead relies on statements from organisations who have a vested interest in pursuing vaccination programs and maintaining "public confidence".

Upon reading the GACVS statement, anyone who had not investigated this matter would think that this vaccine is perfectly safe, yet the truth is far from that as can be seen by the various protest groups, lawsuits, representations to governments and other actions being taken by victims of the HPV vaccines. If the vaccine was perfectly safe, why

> are SO many victims stepping forward and why are many, many doctors, scientists and health professionals trying to get their message heard about the dangers of these vaccines? So in other words, the manufacturers are relying on voluntary reports to reveal adverse reactions 'post marketing'.

To which Professor Herbst responds on December 8th with:

> Dear Ms XXXXX Thank you for your response. I wish to inform you that I am ending our discussion on HPV vaccination. If you have issues around HPV vaccination, I would like to suggest that you take it up with the National Department of Health, and not with the Cancer Association of South Africa.
>
> Kind Regards, Prof Michael C Herbst Health Specialist

Sarah responds almost immediately with (page 39):

> I am saddened and appalled at your response. I am a cancer survivor myself (malignant melanoma) and I am shocked that CANSA refuses to answer genuine concerns about a pharmaceutical product that is supposed to protect against cancer. The general public is led to believe that organisations like CANSA have the best interests of the public at heart but clearly this is not the case.

I therefore wish to place on record the following conclusions that I have drawn from the lack of response by CANSA:

1. CANSA has no interest in protecting the lives of females (or males, as young males are now also being drawn into the HPV vaccination program) in South Africa
2. CANSA is unwilling to properly investigate the flood of reports, scientific studies and documented evidence of the dangers of HPV vaccines
3. CANSA is not providing balanced information to the general public of the dangers of HPV vaccines and therefore has no interest in ensuring full informed consent
4. CANSA refuses to answer my concerns and questions
5. CANSA is putting the lives of all young South Africans at risk by failing to properly investigate the devastating serious adverse effects that are being reported all over the world

As much as Professor Herbst would have liked this to be the end of his conversation about HPV vaccines, it was not meant to be. During the course of Sarah's communications with the director of CANSA, one of the scientists whose work was criticized in Professor Herbst's Dec 6th email had an opportunity to read what the professor had stated. Consequently, Dr. Sin Hang Lee responded directly to Professor Herbst via email [...] on December 11th as follows:

> Dear Professor Herbst:
>
> Based on your 06 December 2015 letter addressed to Ms XXXX on behalf of the Cancer Association of South Africa, you are obviously not a scientist, but are trying to dismiss a very important scientific issue which has affected the health of many teenagers worldwide. Since you are masquerading as a health specialist, acting as a spokesman in a cancer association and trying to discredit my scientific work on the finding of HPV L1 gene DNA in the vaccine Gardasil® while using your position to influence health policy decision making according to your agenda, your letter must not be allowed to pass without challenge.
>
> The first exposure of your lack of understanding of the science involved in this matter is contained in your statement "Several papers have also been published pertaining to the finding of HPV L1 gene DNA fragments in clinical specimens following HPV vaccination [13, 14]. These papers claimed an association with clinical events of an inflammatory nature, including cerebral vasculitis."
>
> You quoted as reference #13 a paper published by "Tomljenovic L, Shaw CA. Death after Quadrivalent Human Papillomavirus (HPV) Vaccination: Causal or Coincidental? Pharmaceut Reg Affairs 2012, S12:001". If you had understood what HPV L1 gene DNA fragments mean, you would not have made such an erroneous statement as you

did because in their entire paper, Tomljenovic and Shaw never mentioned "HPV L1 gene DNA fragments" even once. These authors demonstrated HPV-16L1 VLPs, not DNA fragments in the blood vessel walls. You obviously do not understand the difference between HPV L1 VLPs and HPV L1 gene DNA fragments.

You quoted as reference #14 a paper published by "Lee, SH. Detection of human papillomavirus L1 gene DNA fragments in postmortem blood and spleen after Gardasil® vaccination—A case report. Advances in Bioscience and Biotechnology, 2012, 3, 1214-1224". You are basically putting your words into the author's mouth because I know the author did not claim cerebral vasculitis in this case report.

In an attempt to boost your credibility, your also wrote "*... the case reports* [13] *of adverse events hypothesized to represent a causal association between the HPV L1 gene DNA fragments and death were flawed in both clinical and laboratory methodology* [16]*.*" For reference 16, you cited a CISA Technical report from a U.S. CDC webpage.

However, in this CDC technical report, the unnamed authors of the document only questioned the HPV-16L1 particles, never HPV L1 gene DNA fragments. Therefore, it further confirms the fact that you really do not understand these two important and distinct chemicals in the HPV vaccine at all. And there is a Disclaimer following this document, stating: The information and conclusions in this report are those of the work group participants addressing this issue and do not necessarily represent the official position of CDC. So you blindly misquoted a technical report written by a team of ghost writers to dismiss a potential causal association between the HPV L1 gene DNA fragments and death.

You were unable to find a scientific publication published in a peer-reviewed journal to challenge the plausible mechanism leading to potential harm induced by residual HPV DNA left in the vaccine Gardasil®. So you had to use a blog written by a Dr Helen Petousis-Harris who knows even less than you do on this subject to support your opinion. In her blog (your reference #17), Dr Helen Petousis-Harris did not even cited a single publication of mine, and used some social media articles published on the Internet to attack me by character assassination. Although she had no personal experience on viral DNA research, she was brave enough to declare that the quantity of residual HPV DNA left in the vaccine Gardasil® has no health impacts on the vaccinees. It is unfortunate for the teenagers of this world to have people like you and Dr Helen Petousis-Harris to rely on selling your biased opinions without any scientific evidence of your own to influence health policy decision making. Neither of you has done any work to support your opinions. Neither of you knows what you are talking about. If you want to prove me wrong, please show me a report of the amount of HPV L1 gene DNA fragments (type 16, 11, 18 and 6) which are bound to the aluminum adjuvant, as found in the vaccine

Gardasil® that has been shown to be of no short-term or long-term risk to humans.

Since you have quoted in your reference #12, a paper published by Slade BA, Leidel L, Vellozzi C, Woo EJ, Hua W, et al. Postlicensure safety surveillance for quadrivalent human papillomavirus recombinant vaccine. JAMA. 2009 Aug 19; 302(7):750-7. Let me point out to you that this CDC study shows that among 12,424 reported adverse events following Gardasil® vaccination from June 1, 2006 through December 31, 2008, there were 32 deaths with a mean age of 18 years old, who died 2 to 405 days after the last Gardasil® injection. Medical records and autopsy reports on 20 of the 32 deaths were available for review and confirmed there were 4 unexplained deaths and 6 cardiac-related deaths.

This same report also stated that syncope is the most common adverse reaction after Gardasil® injections and "The reporting rates per100 000 qHPV doses distributed were 8.2 for syncope;"

Syncope is defined as temporary loss of consciousness and posture, described as "fainting" or "passing out." It's usually related to temporary insufficient blood flow to the brain. It most often occurs when the blood pressure is too low (hypotension) and the heart doesn't pump a normal supply of oxygen to the brain.

In view of the high incidence of syncope developed among Gardasil® vaccinees, the FDA Prescribing Information for Gardasil® (qHPV) contains the following Warnings and Precautions:

"Because vaccinees may develop syncope, sometimes resulting in falling with injury, observation for 15 minutes after administration is recommended. Syncope, sometimes associated with tonic-clonic movements and other seizure-like activity, has been reported following vaccination with GARDASIL®. When syncope is associated with tonic-clonic movements, the activity is usually transient and typically responds to restoring cerebral perfusion by maintaining a supine or Trendelenburg position."

So why do Gardasil® vaccinees have a higher rate of syncope as compared to other vaccinees? The ugly truth that you and those agencies you have quoted to support your biased opinions would not like to face may be in the HPV L1 gene DNA fragments when the viral DNA fragments combine with the aluminum adjuvants in the vaccines. To understand this, you really have to spend time to study the history on the science of aluminum adjuvants in vaccination.

Aluminum salts have been used as adjuvants in vaccination empirically to boost immune responses of the host to the protein antigens for many decades. However, the mechanism of the adjuvant effects of aluminum salts has only been recently investigated at the molecular level. It is now generally agreed in the scientific community that aluminum salts used as adjuvants are toxic and always damage the cells of the host at the site of injection, causing a localized inflammation at the vaccination site. This initial cell damage by the aluminum salt is an essential and necessary step to initiate its adjuvant effects because the free host DNA molecules released from the aluminum salt-damaged host cells act as mediators to trigger augmented immune responses of the host [1, 2]. The free DNA molecules of the dying host cells, also referred to as damage-associated molecular patterns (DAMPs) [3] bind the aluminum salt adjuvant at the site of injection, and the resulting DNA/aluminum complexes are phagocytized by the antigen-presenting cells (APCs) and macrophages. It was known as early as 2003, that when bound to aluminum salts as nanoparticles, free DNA molecules undergo dramatic conformational changes and can be introduced into mammalian cells as a means of gene transfection [4]. In vaccination with aluminum adjuvants, the transfected host DNA activates the pathways that would increase their ability to interact productively with antigen-specific CD4 T cells to boost host immune responses [1, 2]. In plain language, free DNA derived from the dying host cells is needed to be carried by aluminum adjuvants into the APCs or macrophages to function as mediators for boosting immune responses in vaccination.

However, the presence of recombinant HPV L1-specific DNA fragments in the vaccine Gardasil® has disrupted this expected normal immunity response platform in vaccination. The HPV DNA molecules, being of a viral origin, are "non-self" microbial products, also referred to as pathogen-associated molecular patterns (PAMPs). The human body's defense system can distinguish the PAMPs from the DAMPs in order to mount an appropriate immune response to either the presence of a pathogen or a tissue damage [3].

The amorphous aluminum hydroxyphosphate sulfate (AAHS) nanoparticles which are expected to bind the free host DNA at the site of vaccine injection can also bind the fragments of HPV L1 gene DNA present in the vaccine Gardasil® [5] through a ligand exchange process between the phosphate groups of the DNA molecule and the hydroxyl groups on the aluminum adjuvant surface, similar to a reaction between phospholipids and AAHS in the recombinant hepatitis B vaccine [6]. In other words, Gardasil® has been furnished with a set of ready-made instant DNA immune "mediators" already in the adjuvant, in the form of a viral DNA/aluminum chemical compound, specifically an HPV L1 gene DNA/AAHS complex. The downstream events after transfection into the human macrophages of these viral DNA fragments which are rarely found in the human genome [7] are quite different from those after the DNA of the dying host cells is introduced into the macrophages. Despite similarities between DNA molecules, mammalian cells have the remarkable ability to distinguish viral DNA from their own DNA. The human macrophages are able to recognize the HPV L1 gene DNA as a 'stranger' and a 'danger' signal, and in response produce many antiviral immune molecules, collectively referred to as type I interferons and pro-inflammatory cytokines [8-10].

Massive systemic production of these type I interferons and pro-inflammatory cytokines induces an antiviral state and protects the host, but it also can contribute to endotoxin lethality and autoimmune diseases [9]. Many of these cytokines are myocardial depressants. The two cytokines that show the greatest cardiovascular effects in animals and humans are tumor necrosis factor (TNF)-α and IL-1α [11]. Administration of recombinant TNF-α in animal models is known to cause hemodynamic changes and even death [11].

Injection of Gardasil® into animals has been shown to induce unusually early strong innate immune responses with quick releases of a variety of cytokines from the macrophages [12]. Injection of HPV DNA/AAHS complexes into the host is also known to induce a strong immune reaction and a strong CD8 T cell response [13]. Based on experiments with other viral DNA molecules, the recombinant HPV L1 gene DNA fragments transfected into human macrophages would also be recognized as "stranger" and "danger" signal, and invariably activate the macrophages to release numerous antiviral cytokines. Many of these cytokines, including TNF-α and IL-1α, are recognized myocardial depressants [14-18]. Hypotensive shock induced by TNF-α has been well documented among animals [19, 20] and humans [21, 22].

This brief review of literature shows that there is a known molecular mechanism to explain why syncope occurs more often in people injected with Gardasil® than with other vaccines, and why certain predisposed vaccinees may suffer a sudden unexpected death as the result of Gardasil® vaccination. You and those who blindly dismiss the potential toxicity of aluminum adjuvant and in particular the toxicity of the newly created HPV L1 gene DNA/AAHS compound for marketing an HPV vaccine should be held responsible for intentionally ignoring the scientific evidence at the expense of public interest.

It is of interest that you mentioned that in June 2013, the GACVS reviewed the concerns arising in Japan in regard to reports described as CRPS in a few cases, and other chronic pain conditions following HPV vaccine. But you apparently purposely avoided mentioning the facts that the Japanese government has suspended its HPV vaccine recommendation since 2014 and that a December 10, 2014 Symposium held by the Japan Medical Association and the Japanese Association of Medical Sciences concluded that HPV vaccines should be promoted only after issues regarding vaccine safety are settled.

In summary, to protect the health of the young children there is an urgent need for open debate of the risks versus benefits of HPV vaccination being recommended or forced onto the 12-year old school girls and boys. A simple declaration of vaccine safety made by some armchair professor like you does not serve the interest of the public.

Sin Hang Lee, MD, F.R.C.P. (C), FCAP
Director, Milford Molecular Diagnostics Laboratory
2044 Bridgeport Avenue, Milford, CT 06460 USA

The following is an excerpt from Professor Herbst's email (link to entire email) reply to Dr. Lee which was sent on December 11th:

I wish to thank you for the information provided by you. I undertake to include your counter arguments

> and other relevant information supplied by you in an updated version of CANSA's Fact Sheet on Human Papilloma Virus Infection and Cancer when our offices re-open on 4 January 2016 and will forward a copy of the updated document to you. I will also google your other research contributions in this regard.

There you have it – one single individual putting forth honest questions and demanding honest, documented answers can make a difference!

If Professor Michael Herbst lives up to his word and alters the CANSA fact sheet on HPV infection and cancer to reflect Dr. Lee's concerns, the women of South Africa will be able to understand the potential risks of HPV vaccines as well as the potential benefits prior to making a decision as to whether or not HPV vaccines are a good addition to their cervical cancer prevention program.

The women of South Africa will be able to exercise their right to informed consent, thanks to Sarah.

1. What do you think about this exchange? Do you think that average people can correctly interpret the medical information included here? Or should they put their trust completely in the doctors who specialize in vaccine safety?

"EVERY LAST ONE: HOW TO FORCE TOTAL VACCINE COMPLIANCE BY CONTROLLING THE CONVERSATION AND ELIMINATING CHOICE," BY LOUISE KUO HABAKUS, FROM *WISE TRADITIONS IN FOOD, FARMING AND THE HEALING ARTS*, SUMMER 2015

We want healthy children. We want a healthy society. But we won't always agree on the road to get there. And that road, paved over with "good intentions," may nonetheless deliver us to the same unfortunate destination.

This brings us to the topic of vaccination. With almost no exceptions, the trifecta of government, industry, and organized medicine want every child vaccinated. To achieve total compliance, they're controlling the conversation and taking away our rights.

Let's roll up our sleeves and get right down to it. When it comes to vaccines, there are two kinds of people in the world. You're probably thinking pro-vaccine and anti-vaccine, right? It's neat and pat, and there's millions of dollars behind this PR campaign. But this singular narrative—parents versus the science—is a false one, carefully shaped for reasons that have nothing to do with vaccines, public health, or children.

So how about those two different kinds of people in the world? A much better way of looking at this is pro- and anti-health freedom. The truth is, when it comes to vaccination—like any other diagnostic, therapeutic, or other medical intervention—it doesn't really matter what

I think or do, and what you think or do. What matters is the freedom to choose.

"REFUSERS" ARE PUTTING US ALL AT RISK

Sound familiar? Parents who refuse to vaccinate endanger us all. Here's some of the arguments we are hearing:

- *USA Today*: Jail "anti-vax" parents.
- *Slate Magazine*: How to Deal with Anti-Vaxxers. Try to persuade them. And if that fails, give them no choice.
- *Fox News*: Dr Manny: Should Obama make vaccines mandatory for all children?
- *Reason.com blog*: Shame and Shun Anti-Vaccine Parents.
- *The Verge*: Vaccine Deniers: inside the dumb, dangerous new fad.

These headlines are everywhere. Mainstream media have been on a rampage since the beginning of 2015. Read enough of these stories and you'd feel pretty comfortable concluding that there's a serious public health problem on our hands. Right? Wrong.

AMERICA VACCINATES ITS CHILDREN

The truth is that America vaccinates its children. Using the Centers for Disease Control and Prevention's own data, I would like to impress upon you that "The Vaccine War," as styled by *Frontline*, isn't about vaccines, public health, or even children. The CDC reports that over 99 percent of children are vaccinated, and 90–95 percent are fully vaccinated.

The median exemption rate is 1.8 percent. They will try to tell you this means that 1.8 percent of children are fully unvaccinated. They think we don't know how to do math.

With over 99 percent of children vaccinated, it's reasonable to assume that most children receive their core vaccines. State health department records bear this out, as shown by an analysis of Vermont's data. An exempted child could be fully vaccinated except for a single dose of chickenpox vaccine, or hepatitis B vaccine. State lawmakers looking to blame parents for rising exemption rates should look in the mirror instead. They will find that rising exemptions are tied to the recent, dramatic increase in the number of mandated "non-core" vaccines, including chickenpox, hepatitis B and flu. Parents are doing their own research and concluding that not all diseases and not all vaccines are the same.

BUT WHAT ABOUT DISNEYLAND?

From late 2014 through April 17, 2015, the date by which the California Department of Public Health determined the outbreak had ended, the agency recorded one hundred thirty-six confirmed cases of measles that started in Disneyland in Orange County, California. Shortly after the first cases were reported, mainstream media proceeded to "freak out."

What the press failed to communicate, however, is the fact that the overhyped Disneyland measles affair was completely unrelated to school vaccine exemption laws.

- It started at an amusement park, not a school.
- It originated from an overseas source, not from an exempted child.

- It affected more adults (56 percent) who are not subject to school vaccine laws.
- It never spread into the state of California let alone the entire United States.

In fact, during the past two years, California's coverage rate for measles vaccination has increased – now at 96.2 percent – while its philosophical exemption rate has fallen by 19 percent. Is the CDC trying to tell us that rising vaccine coverage and declining exemption cause outbreaks? I don't think so.

THEY WANT MORE

Those high compliance rates, in the low- to mid-90th percentile, weren't reached until the 1990s. Public health could give itself a gold star for achieving these rates. But they're not satisfied. They want more.

All fifty states have medical exemptions to mandatory vaccination. This is not the issue at hand. Medical exemptions are not a realistic option for most children. For starters, they're almost impossible to get. The CDC's list of accepted medical contraindications to vaccination is so narrow that a child must be sacrificed, or nearly sacrificed, before a parent learns that the child cannot be vaccinated. The CDC is so clear that most sick and immunocompromised children should be vaccinated that it published "Conditions Commonly Misperceived as Contraindications to Vaccination" lest parents and clinicians falsely assume that the following serious conditions qualify as valid reasons to skip vaccination: fevers greater than one hundred five degrees, immunosuppression, seizures, autoimmune disease and nonvaccine allergies. Not even a family history of injury, death, seizures or sudden infant death syndrome following vaccination will qualify a child for a medical exemption. Even a child who already had a vaccine reaction will have trouble getting an exemption—doctors hate to give them and many refuse outright.

The issue at hand is non-medical or parental vaccine exemptions. According to the National Vaccine Information Center, seventeen states provide for a philosophical exemption, forty-eight states offer a religious exemption, and two states (Mississippi and West Virginia) have no choice at all. This was pre-Disneyland.

And the post-Disneyland response?

State legislatures across the country, propelled by industry lobbyists, are moving to eliminate parental vaccine exemptions, or to restrict them so severely that they are effectively eliminated. Since late last year, parental vaccine exemptions are or have been under fire in eighteen states representing well over half of the US population. During the brief window that I was writing this article, Vermont became the first state in the country to remove a philosophical exemption to compulsory vaccination.

It's not enough that vaccines are mandatory for day care and school admission, and over 99 percent of children are vaccinated. They want to eliminate the idea that you could have a choice. They want every last one.

HERE'S WHAT THEY'RE NOT TELLING YOU

Measles is not deadly.

The CDC reported no measles deaths from the Disneyland cases and told Fox News that there have been no measles deaths in over ten years. (This CDC report, however, lists two deaths, one each in 2009 and 2010.) The World Health Organization states that measles mortality is clinically insignificant.

The official health journal of the US Public Health Service asserts that measles is benign; we've had a stable relationship with measles for centuries; complications are infrequent; fatality is rare; and after contracting measles, immunity is solid and lifelong. And for those who have succumbed to the narrative that the measles vaccine has saved millions of US children's lives, take a look at the chart below from the CDC's Department of Vital Statistics.

There's an untold story about measles that has been suppressed because it doesn't fit today's PR-engineered tale of vaccine triumphalism. The inconvenient truth? Measles deaths in America had declined by over 98 percent and in England by almost 100 percent by the time the measles vaccine was first used. And this huge decline in mortality before a vaccine is brought into use is true of almost every infectious disease for which there is a vaccine on the childhood and adult schedules. In fact, many infectious diseases such as scarlet fever declined to zero mortality without any widespread use of a vaccine.

That's not to say that people aren't dying of infections in the US. They are—to the tune of one hundred thousand per year. They're dying of healthcare-associated infections in hospitals. Many of our hospitals have woefully subpar hygiene and infection prevention practices. Procedures such as meticulous hand hygiene and cleaning of equipment and rooms between patients are known to reduce infections by up to 75 percent.

One hundred thousand deaths and no one is clamoring to legislate mandatory hygiene practices in hospitals.

Zero measles deaths, total PR hysteria, and state governments are poised to legislate away your right to choose.

A MASTER CLASS TO FORCE TOTAL VACCINE COMPLIANCE

Government, industry, and organized medicine have been co-teaching a master class on how to turn one hundred thirty-six cases of measles at Disneyland into a permanent public health emergency and force total vaccine compliance.

Here's their curriculum:

- 1. Commandeer the science using industry-sponsored research, then close the book.
- 2. Claim dominance over women's bodies, medicalize pregnancy, and use fear to compel vaccination.
- 3. Teach parents to ignore the brain damage in children that's all around us. Just realize it's always been there, and understand that we're simply better at seeing it.
- 4. Demonize parents and obliterate the right to choose

They are attempting to control the conversation and force total compliance.

A MASTER CLASS ON HEALTH FREEDOM

Educated citizens, 26 however, know that there's more to this than meets the eye. And any conversation that's worth having is one that goes both ways. We reject their curriculum. It's time for a new master class—one that's about personal responsibility, individual agency and collective advocacy:

- 1. Take back the science for yourself.
- 2. Reassert control over your body—the decisions belong to you.
- 3. Look into the eyes of the children and accept the truth.
- 4. Above all, fight for your rights. Fight for health freedom. Or it will be gone.

Here's my course description on health freedom.

RECLAIM THE AFFIRMATIVE MESSAGE

Who says that industry, government, and organized medicine get to define the narrative? We're not against. We're for. We're for independent science. We're for health freedom. We're for our rights.

GO TO SCHOOL ON HUMAN RIGHTS

UNESCO, the United Nations Education, Scientific, and Cultural Organization, has over one hundred ninety member countries around the world. In 2005, UNESCO drafted the Universal Declaration on Bioethics and Human Rights. It's a foundational document that establishes informed consent as the international human rights standard around the world. I urge you to read it; it's spectacular. Here are some highlights, paraphrased for simplicity:

- Because human beings have a unique capacity to give expression to ethical principles ...
- Because of rapid developments in science and technology ...
- Because we should respect human dignity, and

observe human rights and fundamental freedoms ...

- Because health isn't just about science and technology ...
- Because ethical issues in medicine can affect all of us, from individuals and families, to communities and all of mankind ...
- Because innovations cannot be invoked at the expense of our rights and freedoms ...
- Because a person's identity is comprised of many significant, valuable dimensions, including social, cultural, psychological, and spiritual components ...
- Precisely because of all these magnificent things ...

Any preventive, diagnostic, and therapeutic medical intervention is only to be carried out with the prior, free and informed consent of the person concerned, based on adequate information. The consent should, where appropriate, be expressed and may be withdrawn by the person concerned at any time and for any reason without disadvantage or prejudice. [Article 6 – Consent]

In other words, when it comes to any medical intervention, all human beings must have a choice. No one can do anything to you unless you agree. You must be adequately informed. You can change your mind at any time for any reason. And look carefully ... there's no special exemption for vaccination.

FREEDOM AND TRANSPARENCY

We have the right to know and understand what we're putting into our bodies. This means:

- independent scientific research;
- access to the providers, supplements, and treatment options of our choosing;
- high certification standards; and,
- truth-in-labeling.

We need to be health freedom fighters! Something has been happening over the past thirty years. Health freedom as declined in lockstep with all these vaccine mandates. Mandatory vaccination takes away your health freedom.

WHAT DOES IT MEAN TO BE FREE?

What is freedom? Our founding fathers made clear that government should not come between man and his God and conscience. It's not just about human rights law. Divine law, natural law, and the laws of this land, the United States of America, uphold fundamental freedoms and inalienable rights. These rights cannot be surrendered. They aren't supposed to be voted on. They belong to you and to me.

But governments will try because that's what they do, as any student of history can tell us. They overreach. They attempt to pass bills that sweep too broadly. Today, there are over one hundred bills in thirty-four states seeking to increase vaccine mandates; expand state police powers; facilitate monitoring and enforcement; and eliminate our right to choose.

You may think these bills are about public health and children, but they're not. Many of these bills are attempting to legislate away what's rightfully ours. They're a land grab and nothing less than our bodies and our rights are at stake.

Vaccination is the exception that proves the rule. It lays bare the reality that we do not have health freedom in this country.

INTRODUCING HEALTH FREEDOM ACTION

We're proud to introduce Health Freedom Action, a new 501(c)(4) organization for legislative advocacy, to advance the bills that uphold our rights and to oppose the ones that aim to take them away.

We must organize to assert our rights.

There's one true currency in politics. When you see a large amount of money being spent, you can be sure the politicians don't have the support of the people.

It's time to expand our political center of gravity to promote informed consent and health freedom. We need scale, and consistent and uniform messaging. And we must cross state lines, coordinate across disciplines, and gather our allies.

We have professional knowledge. We need professional infrastructure, including:

- best practices;
- talking points, handouts, letters, flyers
- legislative and legal analysis;
- media coordination and training;
- strategic communications;
- speaker's bureau; and
- political organizing.

Informed consent for vaccination, as for every other medical intervention, is a vital expression of health freedom and human rights.

CONSUMER PROTECTION AMENDMENT

Governments are supposed to regulate the activities of corporations and others who provide products and services to the public. Sometimes they fall short. Sometimes they participate in infringing our rights. The modern consumer protection movement hasn't been around that long—about fifty years or so. It is characterized by nonprofit advocacy groups and grassroots activism. Today, there's a rising chorus of voices about compulsory vaccination.

Are vaccines safe or unsafe? People are angry and confused about mixed signals.
If they're so safe, why are vaccine makers shielded from liability?
If they're so safe, why must governments force people to get them?
If they're so safe, why is there a vaccine injury compensation program?
If they're so safe, why are thousands of people across the US protesting?
If they're so safe, why not let the markets decide?

In 1986, Congress passed the National Childhood Vaccine Injury Act (NCVIA), which gave manufacturers and health care professionals complete immunity from any vaccine injury. Why did the federal government remove the most important consumer protection for safer vaccination? How can governments mandate vaccination and eliminate exemptions after blocking lawsuits against vaccine manufacturers? Why don't most people, lawmakers included, know about this?

Will legislators continue to support the removal from parents of their ultimate right to choose when they understand that the vaccine industry enjoys near total liability protection?

As the controversial bill advances through the California legislature, SB277 has been met with strong and growing public resistance. Thousands have traveled to Sacramento to testify and rally. This citizen movement is drawing attention to the legal implications of the arcane National Childhood Vaccine Injury Act (NCVIA) of 1986.

The Consumer Protection Amendment (CPA) was brought forth in California on May 28, 2015 to strike a balance between vaccine mandates and the absence of vaccine manufacturer liability highlighted by SB277.

CPA gives consumers in California the opportunity to sue vaccine manufacturers in the event of injury or death. It also creates the opportunity to challenge the constitutionality of the federal government's attempts to block any lawsuits against vaccine manufacturers. While urging the adoption of this amendment, supporters uphold their opposition to SB277.

Read more about CPA and our call to action at healthfreedomaction.org. There's no time to waste. Let's be fearless and formidable. Together.

1. What rights does a conscientious objector have to disobey a lawful order?

CHAPTER 5

WHAT THE MEDIA SAY

In 1994, surgeon Andrew Wakefield and his colleagues sent a study of a dozen children, nine of whom were autistic, to *The Lancet*, a British medical journal, suggesting a link between autism and the MMR vaccine. As immunology expert John Rhodes later wrote, "the authors speculated that the [MMR] vaccine was a possible environmental trigger." Vaccine safety pressure groups sprang into action, making similar claims in the media in America and Europe.

Through an investigation by British journalist Brian Deer in 2004, Wakefield was revealed to have been hired to discredit the MMR vaccine. "Where science is concerned, journalists like Brian Deer are rare. Instead we have poor and biased science reporting for sensation-hungry newspapers who spread ill-informed opinions like they were solid gold truths," wrote science writer Darryl Cunningham. "In the twenty-first century, is it too much to ask journalists to do basic fact-checking?

And that editors would assign science stories to reporters who have a knowledge of the subject. Is that too much to ask?"

A free press might be free from government censorship, and able to assign reporters to write on any topic. But even the best editor cannot be simultaneously a scholar of vaccine science, a mind reader able to tell which expert or writer is honest, and a prophet who already knows the entire truth. And while responsible editors might publish fairly covered discussions of sensitive topics like vaccines, social media has no editors to cull misinformation and lies.

"SCIENTISTS CRACK A 50-YEAR-OLD MYSTERY ABOUT THE MEASLES VACCINE," BY MICHAELEEN DOUCLEFF, FROM NPR, MAY 7, 2015

Back in the 1960s, the U.S. started vaccinating kids for measles. As expected, children stopped getting measles.

But something else happened.

Childhood deaths from all infectious diseases plummeted. Even deaths from diseases like pneumonia and diarrhea were cut by half. Scientists saw the same phenomenon when the vaccine came to England and parts of Europe. And they see it today when developing countries introduce the vaccine.

"In some developing countries, where infectious diseases are very high, the reduction in mortality has been up to 80 percent," says Michael Mina, a postdoc in biology at Princeton University and a medical student at Emory University. "So it's really been a mystery — why do children stop dying at such high rates from all these different infections following introduction of the measles vaccine," he says.

Mina and his colleagues think they now might have an explanation. And they published their evidence Thursday in the journal Science.

Now there's an obvious answer to the mystery: Children who get the measles vaccine are probably more likely to get better health care in general — maybe more antibiotics and other vaccines. And it's true, health care in the U.S. has improved since the 1960s.

But Mina and his colleagues have found there's more going on than that simple answer.

The team obtained epidemiological data from the U.S., Denmark, Wales and England dating back to the 1940s. Using computer models, they found that the number of measles cases in these countries predicted the number of deaths from other infections two to three years later.

"We found measles predisposes children to all other infectious diseases for up to a few years," Mina says. And the virus seems to do it in a sneaky way.

Like many viruses, measles is known to suppress the immune system for a few weeks after an infection. But previous studies in monkeys have suggested that measles takes this suppression to a whole new level: It erases immune protection to other diseases, Mina says.

So what does that mean? Well, say you get the chicken pox when you're 4 years old. Your immune system figures out how to fight it. So you don't get it again. But if you get measles when you're 5 years old, it could wipe out the memory of how to beat back the chicken pox. It's like the immune system has amnesia, Mina says.

"The immune system kind of comes back. The only problem is that it has forgotten what it once knew," he says. So after an infection, a child's immune system has to almost start over, rebuilding its immune protection against diseases it has already seen before.

This idea of "immune amnesia" is still just a hypothesis and needs more testing, says epidemiologist William Moss, who has studied the measles vaccine for more than a decade at Johns Hopkins University. But the new study, he says, provides "compelling evidence" that measles affects the immune system for two to three years. That's much longer than previously thought. "Hence the reduction in overall child mortality that follows measles vaccination is much greater than previously believed," says Moss, who wasn't involved in the study.

That finding should give parents more motivation to vaccinate their kids, he says. "I think this paper will provide additional evidence — if it's needed — of the public health benefits of measles vaccine," Moss says. "That's an important message in the U.S. right now and in countries continuing to see measles outbreaks." Because if the world can eliminate measles, it will help protect kids from many other infections, too.

© 2016 National Public Radio, Inc. NPR news report titled "Scientists Crack a 50-Year-Old Mystery About the Measles Vaccine" by Michaeleen Doucleff was originally published on NPR.org on May 7, 2015, and is used with the permission of NPR. Any unauthorized duplication is strictly prohibited.

1. Was this article on a complex medical topic difficult to read? If not, how did this journalist make this complex topic more comprehensible for readers?

"BIG PHARMA—CRONY CAPITALISM OUT OF CONTROL," BY RALPH NADER, FROM *COMMON DREAMS*, NOVEMBER 22, 2014

Two recent news items about the voracious drug industry should call for a supine Congress to arouse itself and initiate investigations about the pay-or-die drug prices that are far too common.

The first item—a page one story in the New York Times—was about the Cystic Fibrosis (CF) Foundation, which fifteen years ago invested $150 million in the biotechnology company Vertex Pharmaceuticals to develop a drug for this serious lung disease.

On November 19, the Foundation reported a return of *$3.3 billion* from that investment. Kalydeco, the drug developed with that investment, is taken daily by CF patients (who can afford it) and is priced at $300,000 a year per patient. Who can pay that price?

The second news release came from the drug industry funded Tufts Center for the Study of Drug Development. The Center's Joseph DiMasi asserts that the cost of developing a new prescription medicine is about $2.558

billion, significantly higher than the previous estimate of $802 million that the Center claimed in 2003.

The drug industry promoters use this ludicrous figure to justify sky-high drug prices for consumers. Unfortunately, the criticism of this inflated number does not receive adequate media attention.

Half of the DiMasi assertion is opportunity costs foregone if the drug company invested its money elsewhere. That cuts his estimate by almost half to $1.395 billion. This maneuver gives "inflation" a new meaning. According to economist James P. Love, founder of Knowledge Ecology International, DiMasi also conveniently ignores government subsidies such as so-called orphan drug tax credits, research grants from the National Institutes of Health and government support of the cost of clinical trials that qualify (see keionline.org).

Mr. Love adds that the drug companies spend "much more on marketing than they do on research and development."

Rohit Malpani, Director of Policy and Analysis of Doctors Without Borders (which received the Nobel Prize in 1999), says that if you believe Tufts' figures, whose alleged data analysis is largely secret, "you probably also believe the Earth is flat."

Mr. Malpani cites GlaxoSmithKline's CEO Andrew Witty himself who says that the figure of a billion dollars to develop a drug is a myth.

Malpani adds that "we know from past studies and the experience of non-profit drug developers that a new drug can be developed for just a fraction of the cost the Tufts report suggests. The cost of developing products is variable, but experience shows that new drugs can be developed for as little as $50 million, or up to $186 million if you take failure into account...not only do taxpayers pay for a very large percentage of industry R&D, but are in fact paying twice because they then get hit with high prices for the drugs themselves."

Mr. Malpani was referring primarily to the U.S., where the drug companies show no gratitude for generous tax credits and taxpayer funded R&D (that they get mostly free.) Add the absence of price controls and you the consumer/patient pay the highest drug prices in the world.

Another largely ignored aspect of the industry's R&D is how much of it is directed to products that match, rather than improve, health outcomes—so-called "me too" drugs that are profitable, but don't benefit patients' health.

Also, the consistently profitable drug industry has been continually unable to restrain its deceptive promotion of drugs and inadequate disclosure of side-effects. About 100,000 Americans die every year from adverse effects of pharmaceuticals. Tens of billions of consumer dollars are wasted on drugs that have side effects instead of drugs for the same ailments with lesser side-effects (see citizen.org/hrg).

During a visit in 2000 with military physicians and scientists at the Walter Reed Army Hospital, I asked how much they spent on R&D to develop their antimalarial drugs and other medicine. The answer: five to ten million dollars per drug, which included clinical testing plus the salaries of the researchers.

This "drug development entity" inside the Department of Defense arose because drug companies refused to invest in vaccine or therapeutic drugs for malaria—then the second leading cause for hospitalizing U.S. soldiers in Vietnam (the first being battlefield injuries). So the military brass decided to fill this void in-house, and with considerable success.

The problem with the stinginess of the coddled private pharmaceutical industry regarding vaccine development continues. Drug resistant tuberculosis and other infectious diseases rampant in developing countries continue to take millions of lives each year. The Ebola epidemic is a current lethal illustration of such neglect.

The survival of many millions of people is too important to be left to the drug companies. For a fraction of what the federal government is wasting on spreading and failing lawless wars abroad, it can expand from the Walter Reed Army Hospital example to become a humanitarian superpower that produces life-saving vaccines and medicines as if the plight of sick people mattered more than windfall profits for Big Pharma.

1. According to this article, why do drug companies not focus on developing vaccines for global pandemics like Ebola?

2. If "Big Pharma" can indeed be corrupt and beholden to money, does this lend more credence to so-called anti-vaxxers' claims?

"OPINION PIECE FOR THE IDAHO STATESMAN, BY LESLIE MANNOKIAN, FROM *WISE TRADITIONS*, SUMMER 2015

Do you rely on our local and national newspapers and media for accurate and honest reporting on the issues that affect all Idahoans? If so, you might want to consider the fact that our newspapers are not reporting on some issues, issues of grave concern to many Idahoans.

Have you read about the CDC whistleblower—a senior scientist from CDC who issued a statement that he and his co-authors (other senior figures at CDC) deliberately omitted data to conceal the link they found between the MMR (measles, mumps and rubella) vaccine and autism?1

Have you read that two former Merck scientists have blown the whistle and are suing vaccine-giant Merck in federal court for fraudulently altering data to make it seem that the mumps portion of their MMR vaccine worked in 95 percent of recipients in order to retain their license from FDA when they knew it did not?[2]

Have you read that the National Vaccination Compensation Program has compensated eighty-three cases of acknowledged vaccine-induced brain damage, which include autism, but federal health officials still claim vaccines don't cause autism?[3]

If you haven't read about these cases in our newspapers or seen coverage of these stories in other media, perhaps that is because the pharmaceutical industry is the largest advertiser today, spending billions every year, and these media outlets don't want to bite the hand that feeds them. Or perhaps those running these media outlets are afraid of the truth.

Either way, we want to share with you the opinion piece we submitted to the *Idaho Statesman*. This piece is largely the same as an opinion piece we sent to the *Idaho Mountain Express* in response to inaccurate and misleading opinion pieces run by both newspapers. Unfortunately, neither of our opinion pieces was published.

We were very disappointed at this seeming censorship, in particular because our opinion pieces were supported by over thirty citations from published, peer-reviewed scientific literature. *The Idaho Statesme*n stated that they were afraid the opinion piece might frighten parents. We would say that parents are already frightened because they do not feel they are being told the truth by federal health agencies or the media and our experience would suggest that is true.

Following is our fully-referenced opinion piece:

The *Idaho Statesman's* opinion piece on vaccines stopped short of advocating mandatory vaccines but stated that parents should not "expect to take advantage of a public education if you are unwilling to participate in sound public health precautions." Given that most parents do not have the resources to home-school, this amounts to a call for forced vaccination.

The assumption that "sound public health advice" is absolute is quite worrying. After all, one-size-fits-all is never appropriate with any pharmaceutical product—but public health officials say this is the case with vaccines. Nor is science infallible. Indeed for decades federal health officials have advised reducing dietary saturated fats and emphasizing carbohydrates, but recent science has proven how dangerous that advice can be.[4] What is sound advice today may not be so sound tomorrow. Add to this the fact that properly prescribed FDA approved drugs kill over one hundred thousand Americans every year and that drug companies have paid thirty billion dollars in fines for repeated fraud, and it's no wonder why some folks question "sound public health advice" and want to decide for themselves what is best for their own families.[5,6]

Though it is commonly believed that vaccines are safe for all but a very few, abundant science proves this assertion false. In producing and screening our award-winning documentary on vaccines, "The Greater Good," we met dozens of scientists who had published studies concerning adverse vaccine reactions, interviewed dozens of doctors who expressed reservations about vaccine safety, and met thousands of families whose children were injured or died after vaccination.

All too often scientists and doctors who acknowledge vaccine risks are demonized and marginalized with the threat of losing their medical licenses.[7] And caring, educated parents who research vaccine safety for themselves, often after having a child suffer vaccine injury, are dismissed as ill-informed, anti-vaccine crazies, but nothing could be further from the truth.

Opinion polls show that vaccine safety is of concern to most American parents and that those who question vaccine safety are mostly highly educated, affluent folks.[8,9,10]

It is often stated that vaccines are irrefutably safe. Why, then, does US law recognize vaccines can injure and kill?[11] Why has the Vaccine Injury Compensation Program (VICP) paid out over three billion dollars to victims?[12] Why do many receive gag orders? Why does VICP list death, anaphylaxis, brain damage and related seizures, and mental impairment as compensable vaccine injuries?[13] Why has the Supreme Court determined that vaccines are "unavoidably unsafe?"[14] Why are vaccine makers shielded from liability for vaccines?[15,16] Why does government maintain the Vaccine Averse Events Reporting System to track vaccine injuries?[17] Why do Glaxo-SmithKline's internal documents show children develop autism after its vaccine Infarix?[18]

The question we should all be asking is why have one hundred fifty cases of measles in a nation of over three hundred million people garnered virtual nonstop media attention for weeks and prompted the introduction of legislation nationwide to restrict vaccine exemptions?

Could the frenzy be a diversion from looming Congressional hearings investigating claims of CDC whistleblower Dr William Thompson, a senior scientist, that he and CDC officials omitted data from a study over a decade ago to conceal the link between the MMR vaccine and autism?[19] Or perhaps lawsuits against vaccine giant Merck alleging Merk management and scientists fraudulently concealed the fact that Merck's MMR vaccine is not as effective as claimed?[20] Or perhaps the abject failure of this year's flu vaccine, merely [23] percent effective?[21]

Media coverage of measles cases and vaccine exemptions suggests an emergency over measles, but the true emergency is the failing health of our nation's children with 54 percent suffering from an autoimmune disease or neurodevelopmental disability, which science links to vaccines.[22,23] Although US children are the most heavily vaccinated in the world, thirty-three developed nations have lower infant mortality rates. Contrast this with zero deaths from measles in ten years but one hundred eight deaths reported after MMR vaccines.[24]

The media routinely blame unvaccinated individuals for recent disease outbreaks, but most of those who contracted mumps, pertussis, or measles in the majority of recent outbreaks were vaccinated, and nations with vaccination rates of 97-99 percent still suffer outbreaks.[25,26] The true culprit is vaccine failure, as vaccine-induced immunity is not permanent.[27,28,29, 30] In addition, science shows vaccinated individuals can and do carry and spread disease, and hospitals warn immuno-compromised patients to avoid those recently vaccinated.[31,32,33,34,35,36] (Please note that since writing this letter, both St Jude's and Johns Hopkins removed their website warning to the immuno-compromised to avoid those recently vaccinated with live virus vaccines.)

We all want to live in as safe a society as possible, but how can anyone argue that any pharmaceutical product is safe for all, or that we know what is best for others? What's next? Should we ban from public places those who eat sugar and junk food, foods that undermine our immune systems, or those with a cough from leaving home? Do we really want to cede ownership of our bodies to the state? I don't.

Find links to two hundred published studies here: greatergoodmovie.org/learn-more/science/

1. Is this article more convincing than other articles? Why or why not?

2. Why do you think newspapers refused to publish this article?

"DEAR PARENTS, YOU ARE BEING LIED TO," BY JENNIFER RAFF, FROM VIOLENT METAPHORS

In light of recent outbreaks of measles and other vaccine preventable illnesses, and the refusal of anti-vaccination advocates to acknowledge the problem, I thought it was past time for this post.

Dear parents,

You are being lied to. The people who claim to be acting in the best interests of your children are putting their health and even lives at risk.

They say that measles isn't a deadly disease.
But it is.

They say that chickenpox isn't that big of a deal.
But it can be.

They say that the flu isn't dangerous.
But it is.

They say that whooping cough isn't so bad for kids to get.
But it is.

They say that vaccines aren't that effective at preventing disease.
But 3 million children's lives are saved every year by vaccination, and 2 million die every year from vaccine-preventable illnesses.

They say that "natural infection" is better than vaccination.
But they're wrong.

They say that vaccines haven't been rigorously tested for safety.
But vaccines are subjected to a higher level of scrutiny than any other medicine. For example, a study tested the safety and effectiveness of the pneumococcal vaccine in more than 37,868 children.

They will say that doctors won't admit there are any side effects to vaccines.
But the side effects are well known, and except in very rare cases quite mild.

They say that the MMR vaccine causes autism. It doesn't. (The question of whether vaccines cause autism has been investigated in study after study, and they all show overwhelming evidence that they don't.)

They say that thimerosal in vaccines causes autism. It doesn't, and it hasn't been used in most vaccines since 2001 anyway.

They say that the aluminum in vaccines (an adjuvant, or component of the vaccine designed to enhance the body's immune response) is harmful to children. But children consume more aluminum in natural breast milk than they do in vaccines, and far higher levels of aluminum are needed to cause harm.

They say that the Vaccine Adverse Events Reporting System (and/or the "vaccine court") proves that vaccines are harmful.
It doesn't.

They say that the normal vaccine schedule is too difficult for a child's immune system to cope with.
It isn't.

They say that if other people's children are vaccinated, there's no need for their children to get vaccinated.

This is one of the most despicable arguments I've ever heard. First of all, vaccines aren't always 100% effective, so it is possible for a vaccinated child to still become infected if exposed to a disease. Worse, there are some people who can't receive vaccinations, because they are immune deficient, or because they are allergic to some component. Those people depend upon herd immunity to protect them. People who choose not to vaccinate their children against infectious diseases are putting not only their own children at risk, but also other people's children.

They say that "natural," "alternative" remedies are better than science-based medicine.
They aren't.

The truth is that vaccines are one of our greatest public health achievements, and one of the most important things you can do to protect your child.

I can predict exactly the sort of response I will be getting from the anti-vaccine activists. Because they can't argue effectively against the overwhelming scientific evidence about vaccines, they will say that I work for Big Pharma. (I don't and never have.) They will say that I'm not a scientist (I am), and that I'm an "Agent 666" (I don't know what that is, but I'm pretty sure that I'm not one).

None of these things are true, but they are the reflexive response by the anti-vaccine activists because they have no facts to back up their position. On some level, deep down, they must understand this, and are afraid of the implications, so they attack the messenger.

Why are they lying to you? Some are doing it for profit, trying to sell their alternative remedies by making you afraid of science-based medicine. I'm sure that many others within the anti-vaccine movement have genuinely good intentions, and do honestly believe that vaccines are harmful. But as a certain astrophysicist recently said "The good thing about science is that it's true whether or not you believe in it." In the case of vaccine truthers, this is not a good thing. Good intentions will not prevent microbes from infecting and harming people, and the message that vaccines are dangerous is having dire consequences. There are outbreaks of vaccine-preventable illnesses now throughout the United States because of unvaccinated children.

In only one respect is my message the same as the anti-vaccine activists: Educate yourself. But while they mean "Read all these websites that support our position", I suggest you should learn what the scientific community says. Learn how the immune system works. Go read about the history of disease before vaccines, and talk to older people who grew up when polio, measles, and other diseases couldn't be prevented. Go read about about how vaccines are developed, and how they work. Read about Andrew Wakefield, and how his paper that claimed a link between the MMR vaccine and autism has been withdrawn, and his medical license has been revoked. Read the numerous, huge studies that have explicitly examined whether autism is caused by the vaccine ... and found nothing. (While you're at it, read about the ongoing research to determine what IS the cause—or causes—of autism, which is not helped by people continuing to insist that vaccines cause it).

That may seem like a lot of work, and scientific papers can seem intimidating to read. But reading scientific articles is a skill that can be mastered. Here's a great resource for evaluating medical information on the internet, and I wrote a guide for non-scientists on how to read and understand the scientific literature. You owe it to your children, and to yourself, to thoroughly investigate the issue. Don't rely on what some stranger on the internet says (not even me!). Read the scientific studies that I linked to in this post for yourself, and talk to your pediatricians. Despite what the anti-vaccine community is telling you, you don't need to be afraid of the vaccines. You should instead be afraid of what happens without them.

"Humans try to make sense of the world by seeing patterns. When they see a disease or condition that tends to appear around the time a child is a year or so old, as autism does, and that is also the age that kids get particular shots, they want to put those things together. Parents watch

kids more carefully after they get shots. Sometimes they pick up on symptoms then. Just because two things happen at the same time doesn't mean that one caused the other. This is why we need careful scientific studies."

1. Does this article, in your opinion, succeed at refuting previous articles that argue that vaccines are dangerous? Why or why not?

"THE DANGERS OF VACCINE DENIAL," BY NICOLAS KRISTOF, FROM THE *NEW YORK TIMES*, FEBRUARY 8, 2015

IN a few backward parts of the world, extremists resist universal childhood vaccinations. The Taliban *in tribal areas of Pakistan. Boko Haram militants in Northern Nigeria.*

Oh, yes, one more: *Some politicians in the United States.*

Senator Rand Paul — a doctor! — told CNBC that he had delayed his own children's immunizations and cited "many tragic cases of walking, talking, normal children who wound up with profound mental disorders after vaccines."

After an uproar, Paul walked back his remarks and tweeted a photo of himself getting a Hepatitis A vaccination. After that irresponsible scaremongering, I'd say he deserves to get shots daily for a decade. With really long needles.

Gov. Chris Christie of New Jersey weighed in as well, suggesting that vaccinations are partly a matter of family choice — before later seeming to retreat as well. Paul and Christie are Republicans, but public health illiteracy is bipartisan: Vaccination rates are particularly low in some liberal Democratic enclaves in California.

At the Waldorf Early Childhood Center in Santa Monica, Calif., 68 percent of the children had "personal belief exemptions" to avoid vaccination requirements, according to The Hollywood Reporter (the school declined to comment). That suggests that kids in some wealthy areas are as well vaccinated as children in, say, Somalia.

President Obama made ambiguous remarks in 2008 that also seemed to suggest that the science is inconclusive about a link between vaccines and autism. And Hillary Rodham Clinton suggested the same thing that year. (Since then, both have emphasized strong support for vaccines.)

Let's call this out as the nonsense it is. If we're going to denounce the Taliban for blocking polio vaccinations, we should be just as quick to stand up to health illiteracy in our midst.

First, a word on vaccines: They have revolutionized public health.

Can you name the discoverer of the smallpox vaccine? Probably not: Edward Jenner is little known today. He lived roughly when Napoleon did, and (by my back-of-envelope calculations) he managed before he died to save many millions more lives than Napoleon cost in his wars over the same period.

All told, up to the present, Jenner's vaccine appears to have saved more than half a billion lives since 1800, notes Dr D.A. Henderson, who led the effort to eradicate smallpox. Jenner should be counted as one of the great heroes of the modern world, yet he is forgotten while everybody knows of Napoleon. That's emblematic of the way vaccines get short shrift.

In reporting on poverty worldwide, I've seen how much vaccines improve human well-being. I understand how troglodytes in the Taliban or Boko Haram can be suspicious of vaccines, but politicians here in affluent, well-educated America? Moms and dads in Santa Monica?

Granted, for a time, it was plausible to wonder about a possible link between vaccines and autism, based on a 1998 article in *The Lancet*, the British medical journal. But that report was quickly discredited by at least 13 studies, and it was retracted in 2010. The author has been stripped of his medical license.

In Britain, for example, researchers found no change in the rate of autism diagnosis after the 1987 introduction of the M.M.R. vaccine against measles, mumps and rubella, and M.M.R. vaccination rates were similar for autistic children and for others. Likewise, studies in California and Atlanta found no correlation between autism rates and M.M.R. vaccinations. Japan suspended the M.M.R. vaccine because of health concerns, yet a careful study found that autism continued to rise.

Dr Philip J. Landrigan, the chairman of the department of preventive medicine at the Mount Sinai medical school, says that there may be environmental factors linked to autism, but these relate to endocrine disrupting chemicals in consumer products, not to vaccines.

"Rather than worry about a vaccine-autism connection that has been proven not to exist, parents should be banding together and writing their elected officials to insist that chemicals be properly tested for toxicity to children before they are allowed to enter the American market," Dr. Landrigan told me. "The Europeans have passed such legislation. We should, too."

Yet American parents remain fixated on vaccines in ways that endanger children. According to the World Health Organization, the measles vaccination rate in 2013 stood at 91 percent in the United States — lower than in Zimbabwe or Bangladesh.

Senator Paul and Governor Christie seemed, initially at least, sympathetic to a "personal choice" argument that parents should be allowed to endanger their children in some circumstances. But that's not the issue here.

The point of immunization isn't just to protect your own child, but also to protect others. Especially those like Rylee Beck, a 5-year-old girl in Orange, Calif., who is fighting leukemia and can't be vaccinated. To stay safe, she depends on others getting vaccinated and creating "herd immunity" to keep the disease at bay.

"Rylee is in pre-K, and it's a scary thing sending her there every day," her mother, Melissa Beck, told me. In December, the family took Rylee to Disneyland and then was terrified when a measles outbreak infected visitors to the park at that time.

"It just scared us to death," Melissa Beck said. "We were just holding our breath, hoping nothing was going to come out of it." Fortunately, Rylee was not infected.

It's not just cancer patients who can't be immunized, but also infants, those with vaccine allergies, and people with medical conditions that leave them immunocompromised. And a small proportion of people get the vaccine but never develop immunity, so they, too, depend on others to get vaccinated.

Thus refusing to vaccinate your children is not "personal choice" but public irresponsibility. You no more have the right to risk others by failing to vaccinate than you do by sending your child to school with a hunting knife. Vaccination isn't a private choice but a civic obligation.

Melissa Beck says that other parents are universally kind and helpful when they see Rylee, frail and sometimes without hair, and learn that she is fighting cancer. She's sure that other parents aren't deliberately putting children like Rylee at risk; they just don't know better.

"It's a matter of life and death for these kids," Melissa said. "Maybe that would change these parents' minds."

1. When a writer takes a personal and informal tone, does it matter to readers if she or he is published in a highly respected newspaper or self-published on a blog?

CHAPTER 6

WHAT ORDINARY CITIZENS SAY

While health care workers complain about anti-vaccine rhetoric by uninformed people in the media and on social media, activists are complaining that doctors and government officials are not listening to their concerns. "We've come to a crossroads," notes Dr. Paul Offit. "And the questions have gotten harder." People can be bewildered by unfamiliarity with symptoms of diseases that are no longer common. It doesn't help that a one-in-a-million risk statistic adds up in a world with over seven billion people.

"A study showed that parents judged symptoms following vaccination as more severe than when the very same symptoms occurred during a disease," wrote the European Centre for Disease Prevention and Control. People "tend to regret negative outcomes that result from their own actions more—because they feel guilty—than when the same outcomes occur due to inaction—because it's fate. Understanding this bias can help to make less biased decisions." Experience does not have to be our only teacher.

"THE IMMUNE SYSTEM: A PAPER FOR UNIVERSITY EXTENSION COURSE UNI 201," BY LYNDA BOYD

This paper will highlight the importance of proper hand washing, immunization shots, the role of a mother's healthy immune system, and the difference between communicable and noncommunicable diseases as taught by professor Ed Ishiguro.

The immune system presentation by professor Ed Ishiguo has not only been informative but also persuasive as it convinced me, as I hope to convince you, about the importance of proper hand washing and getting vaccinations to prevent certain diseases. As well, it has helped me to understand how a mother's healthy immune system can benefit her newborn from developing some serious diseases. And lastly, I learned to distinguish between communicable diseases and noncommunicable diseases and why it is important to wash one's hands correctly if one is to help protect oneself against contracting a bacterial infection or viral disease.

Regarding hand washing: I am one of "those" who unfortunately had to deal with the effects of overuse of antibiotics (drugs that kill bacteria and fungi) to combat recurrent bladder infection and then have to deal with nasty *Clostridium difficil*e. When one antibiotic does not do the job then another stronger one is used. Unfortunately, it can leave the door wide open to contract a serious disease as certain bacteria are becoming more and more resistant to some antibiotics. Antibiotics not only wipe out the unhealthy bacteria but also the healthy bacteria. It leaves one's digestive system in a mess. I ended up having to avoid many foods and ingest great quantities of probiotics (healthy bacteria such as lactobacillus found in yogurt, or bought in capsule or liquid form). Getting the gut flora back to a healthy balance is challenging.

Proper hygiene is important. Washing one's hands properly and often and for 20 seconds with soap after handling foods, pets, etc. and especially after going to the washroom or if you are spending time with someone who is ill or in the beginning stages of illness as simple as a cold, is one way in preventing problems [sp].

As well it is not a good idea to cough or sneeze into one's hand [sp]. I only have to listen to the latest recall of produce due to harmful bacteria found or see someone sneeze into her hands at a grocery store, pick up and then put down a vegetable, to convince me to wash the vegetables thoroughly and to avoid shaking hands with someone who has coughed or sneezed into his hand.

Regarding bacterial infections: Older friends of mine who ended up in the hospital from a simple cut which developed into a Staphylococcal infection (singlecelled parasitic organism) due to complications with fluid in the lungs is additional evidence that these germs are getting more difficult to deal with. According to Dr. Ishiguro, the thymus decreases in size as we get older and so there are not as many T cells to deal with infections. As T cells are the cells that provide immunity as do B cells, which are found in the lymph nodes, spleen, and are distributed in the blood. The B and T cells bind to antigens resulting in these foreign bodies inability to invade.

Although antibodies attack and dismantle harmful pathogens (germs that cause disease), Staphylococcus may gain an upper hand when there is an insufficient response by the immune system. The individual may require intravenous antibiotics or may need additional treatment for respiratory problems.

Antibodies or immunoglobulins such as IgM found on membranes of B cells, IgA found on lining of intestinal tract and bronchial tract as well as saliva and tears, IgE in the allergic response, and IgD found in blood, block tissue invasion and watch for foreign matter while providing immunity.

Phagocytes (white blood cells or leukocytes) can engulf bacteria or other invading microorganisms as an army would attack the enemy. Our part in helping our defense system comes when we get immunized.

Regarding immunization: I may not have been a proponent of getting an immunization shot before but I am now. It is quick and easy and will prevent one from getting a communicable disease like shingles (virus in adults) that can develop many years later after one has had chickenpox. It is hard to get over and causes a lot of pain. Some friends developed it in their eyes, ears and mouth and that was enough information for me to want to protect myself against shingles as my immune system is not what it used to be.

Protecting myself against Human Papillomavirus (HPV) and hepatitis became important after I heard Professor Ishiguro speak about these two diseases and the importance of getting immunized against them to prevent cancer. My mother had hepatitis and my sister died of cervical cancer and these two occurrences in one's family suggest that it is important to be immunized even if one is over 45. The HPV is a shot both young men and women who are sexually active ought to get to prevent cancer in the future.

Regarding allergies and sensitivities: When I was younger, bee stings or kiwi did not result in an allergic reaction because my body did not see it as an enemy. However, as I aged it did and sent out the army to attack. I developed a severe reaction to bee stings and kiwi which resulted in my carrying an Epipen so that my respiratory system would not shut down in the body's attempt to destroy the enemy. IgA and IgE immunoglobulins are proteins produced in our body that go after certain antigens (foreign bodies). The intestines, mucous, saliva, or tears signal to us in the form of sneezing, tingling, or swelling that there is a possible allergic reaction.

There are quite a few allergens (a substance that could cause an allergic reaction) that will cause me to sneeze but does not lead to anaphylactic shock where my breathing could shut down due to the exaggerated defense response by my immune system. These allergens cause enough of an inflammatory response problem in my body, though, and so I try to stick to a diet provided by the nutritionist as well as drink plenty of water.

Regarding a healthy immune system: Mother passes onto the fetus, if we are lucky enough to have healthy mothers, an amazing defense system. The baby receives from the mother immunoglobulins IgM and IgG. IgM and IgG attack harmful microbes or microorganisms such as bacteria, viruses, yeasts.

Another slower system, the acquired, then remembers the disease. The child can gain immunity from certain diseases afterward from being immunized or if he or she contracts a disease early on in life. If an infant receives scheduled immunization shots, though, it would be protected against a host of diseases in a less severe manner than by developing it by contracting it from another person.

It may seem insignificant but if someone does not get immunized against measles and develops it, he or she could be responsible for infecting other individuals who have not been immunized against measles which in turn could detrimentally affect a population. This happened in a community in B.C.[British Columbia] in 2014 that decided against immunization.

Regarding communicable diseases and noncommunicable diseases: For example Ebola, flu, hepatitis, C. *difficile,* AIDS, and now the newest, Zika virus (that affects a fetus, producing deformed babies) transmitted by the bite of a mosquito and which could possibly be transmitted via sexual intercourse [sp]. These are communicable diseases; whereas *Staphylococcus* infection or *Clostridium tetani* (Tetanus) are bacterial infections and are noncommunicable diseases.

I would not want myself nor anyone else to get any communicable or noncommunicable diseases and so want people to wash their hands (with soap) for 20 seconds, get immunized especially if their birth mothers were not that healthy, and cover mouths when sneezing or coughing to assist the immune system against its fight against communicable and noncommunicable diseases.

There was much, much more that Professor Ishiguro presented, but for me, the above information stood out. I am very grateful for his lecture on immunology as I have a much better understanding of disease. I understand how my body responds to an attack by a foreign body and the makeup of the army that defends against such an attack. Finally, I understand why and how to take better care of myself. I hope the above information has been of help to you as well.

1. Where can people who aren't medically trained turn for help in making decisions about vaccination?

"CALIFORNIA, CAMELOT AND VACCINES," BY FRANK BRUNI, FOR THE *NEW YORK TIMES*, JULY 4, 2015

If you had told me a while back that I'd someday dread, dodge and elect not to return phone calls from a prominent member of the Kennedy dynasty, I would have said you were nuts.

Then Robert Kennedy Jr. started reaching out.

Not just reaching out, mind you, but volunteering to educate me. To illuminate me. That was his tone of voice, somewhat pitying and vaguely patronizing, the one time we talked at length, after he'd left messages and before he left more.

It was important, he said, that we meet.

If we did, he said, he could correct me.

My error?

I had disparaged the alarmists who claim a connection between vaccines and autism and fill parents with needless fears about immunizing their children.

I had sided with the American Medical Association, the American Academy of Pediatrics, the National Institutes of Health and the Centers for Disease Control and Prevention. Kennedy knew better.

Lucky for the rest of us, Jerry Brown doesn't.

He did something last week that more governors should, signing legislation that compels almost all schoolchildren in California to be vaccinated.

While the state had been fairly liberal in granting exemptions to parents who cited strongly held personal beliefs, the new law insists that there be a sound medical reason for opting out. Some children with compromised immune systems, for example, simply cannot be given the shots.

I imagine that Kennedy was displeased. I'll confine myself to imagining, because I'm not about to hop on the phone with him again. He'd just subject me to the scaremongering he practiced in his campaign against the California law.

"They can put anything they want in that vaccine and they have no accountability for it," he told an audience in April, according to *The Sacramento Bee*, casting the C.D.C. and drug companies as shadowy peddlers of toxins that ruin children's lives.

Of those children, he added: "They get the shot, that night they have a fever of a hundred and three, they go to sleep, and three months later their brain is gone. This is a holocaust, what this is doing to our country."

Their brain is gone?

A holocaust?

If only we had vaccines against hysteria and hyperbole.

It's tempting just to ignore Kennedy, who later apologized for the word "holocaust," and his fellow vaccine opponents.

But they keep pressing their case, muttering about cover-ups by the government and "big pharma," trying to make sure that California isn't the start of something. (Only two other states, Mississippi and West Virginia, are as strict about vaccines.)

And they're the epitome of the sloppy talk, selfishness and disingenuousness too common in our debate and society.

One of Kennedy's comrades in arms is the actor Jim Carrey, whose anti-vaccine theology apparently took form and flight in the church of Jenny McCarthy, his onetime romantic partner and the high priestess of anti-vaccine conspiracy theorists.

A week ago Carrey tweeted: "Greed trumps reason again as Gov Brown moves closer to signing vaccine law in Cali. Sorry kids. It's just business."

How predictable: When you don't have scientific consensus on your side, shout "greed." Invoke the boogeyman of unbridled capitalism.

Never mind that it's nonsense. As Phil Plait wrote

in Slate last week, there's odd logic to "the claim that somehow pharmaceutical companies make huge amounts of money on vaccines. Actually, if money were the only reason they did this, it would be far more profitable for those companies to let people get sick." The profits from continuing treatments would be considerable.

After Brown indeed signed the law, Carrey tweeted that "California Gov says yes to poisoning more children with mercury and aluminum" and that "this corporate fascist must be stopped."

As it happens, aluminum isn't present in all vaccines and not all mercury is created equal and equally risky.

And *fascist?* Carrey has obviously done worship in the church of Robert Kennedy Jr., too.

The anti-vaccine crowd's bloated language is matched by its narcissism. The whole reason that parents in this paranoid tribe can deem the risk of not immunizing their children acceptable is that they're counting on other parents *to* immunize their children and thus create the so-called herd immunity that's the whole point of mandatory vaccinations.

They want the freedom to do as they please but don't really want everyone else to emulate them, because then measles and mumps and whooping cough would be immediate threats that eclipse the lesser — indeed, the *imagined* — threat of vaccine-induced autism. The anti-vaccine crowd depends on others to comply so that they can hallucinate.

Kennedy's fixation on vaccines goes back about a decade and is in some ways related to his advocacy for the environment. A concern about mercury emissions from industrial plants led to a concern about mercury in thimerosal, a vaccine preservative. He has promoted the idea of a link between thimerosal and autism. The problem isn't just that most respectable scientists reject any such connection, but also that thimerosal has been removed from — or reduced to trace amounts in — most childhood vaccines.

The anti-vaccine agitators can always find a renegade researcher or random "study" to back them up. This is erudition in the age of cyberspace: You surf until you reach the conclusion you're after. You click your way to validation, confusing the presence of a website with the plausibility of an argument.

Although the Internet could be making all of us smarter, it makes many of us stupider, because it's not just a magnet for the curious. It's a sinkhole for the gullible.

It renders everyone an instant expert. You have a degree? Well, I did a Google search!

Vaccine opponents are climate-change deniers with less gluten and more Prada, chalking up the fact that they're in a minority to the gutless groupthink of the majority.

They've learned that as soon as you allege collusion and conspiracy, you've come up with a unified theory that explains away all opposition and turns your lonely stance into a courageous one.

And they're not honest about their fulminations.

Kennedy has insisted that he's "very much pro-vaccine," noting that his six children were vaccinated. He's just trying to ensure that vaccines are safe, he says.

But that means that he thinks that they're dangerous, and there's one message above all others to be taken from his rant about mass destruction and from statements like this one, which he made on a radio show in 2011: "I can see that this fraud is doing extraordinary damage to the brains of American children."

He's telling parents to watch out. He's giving them license not to protect children from preventable illnesses.

That's inarguably anti-vaccine. It's seriously irresponsible. And it's especially sad coming from someone whose family's legend — more Camelot than crackpot — means that he gets crowds to listen to him, lawmakers to meet with him and most of his calls returned.

1. Does writing for a newspaper's opinion column give a journalist the right to speak more frankly about someone's opinions than in a front-page article?

"5 FACTS ABOUT VACCINES IN THE U.S.," BY MONICA ANDERSON, FROM THE PEW RESEARCH CENTER, JULY 17, 2015

California Gov. Jerry Brown signed legislation June 30 making it mandatory as of next July for children enrolled in public or private schools and day cares to be vaccinated, ending the state's policy that allowed personal and religious exemptions to vaccine requirements. The new law, one of the strictest in the nation, comes after a measles outbreak in California infected more than 100 and prompted health officials to urge parents to properly vaccinate their children.

The outbreak and subsequent legislation has brought new attention to the anti-vaccination movement, vaccine safety and mandatory immunizations. Here are five facts about the issue:

1. A VAST MAJORITY OF AMERICANS VIEW CHILDHOOD VACCINES AS SAFE.

Roughly eight-in-ten U.S. adults (83%) say vaccines for diseases such as measles, mumps and rubella are safe for healthy children, according to a Pew Research Center survey conducted earlier this year. Only 9% of the public say these types of vaccines are unsafe, while 7% say they don't know.

2. ALTHOUGH MAJORITIES OF ALL MAJOR DEMOGRAPHIC GROUPS SAY VACCINES ARE SAFE, SOME GROUPS ARE MORE SKEPTICAL THAN OTHERS.

Younger adults are more likely than older adults to believe vaccines are harmful. Some 12% of adults ages 18 to 49 say childhood vaccinations are unsafe, while only 5% of adults 50 and older agree. There are also differences based on race and educational attainment. Blacks (26%) and Hispanics (15%) are more likely than whites (6%) to say childhood vaccinations are unsafe. And 14% of those with a high school diploma or less believe that vaccines are unsafe, compared with just 6% of those with some college experience or more.

3. ROUGHLY TWO-THIRDS OF AMERICAN ADULTS SUPPORT MANDATORY CHILDHOOD VACCINATIONS, BUT YOUNGER ADULTS ARE MORE LIKELY TO SAY VACCINATING CHILDREN SHOULD BE A PARENTAL CHOICE.

A Pew Research survey conducted in 2014 found that 68% of U.S. adults agree that all children should be required to be vaccinated, while 30% say vaccinating children should be a parental choice. These overall views have changed little since 2009, when 69% of the public said childhood vaccinations should be required.

Yet while opinions on this issue were similar across age groups in 2009, the 2014 survey shows that younger adults are more likely to support parental choice: 41% of 18- to 29-year-olds believe parents should have the right not to vaccinate their children, compared with only 20% of adults ages 65 or older. While there are no significant differences on this question by race, education, income or gender, a multivariate logistic regression analysis finds that more Hispanics tend to say vaccines should be required compared with non-Hispanic whites.

4. DEMOCRATS ARE SOMEWHAT MORE LIKELY THAN REPUBLICANS OR INDEPENDENTS TO SAY CHILDHOOD VACCINATIONS SHOULD BE REQUIRED.

While similar shares of Republicans, Democrats and independents agree that vaccines are safe for healthy children, there are modest divisions on the question of whether or not vaccines should be required. Republicans

(34%) and independents (33%) are somewhat more likely than Democrats (22%) to believe that vaccinating children should be a parental choice. In 2009, there were no differences based on party affiliation.

5. ONLY THREE STATES – MISSISSIPPI, WEST VIRGINIA AND NOW CALIFORNIA – DO NOT ALLOW RELIGIOUS OR PERSONAL EXEMPTIONS TO VACCINES.

With the new legislation, California will join Mississippi and West Virginia as the only states that do not offer non-medical exemptions for childhood vaccinations, according to a Pew Research analysis of state laws. In all, 46 states allow religious exemptions for childhood vaccines, while 17 states allow both personal and religious exemptions. In Maine, a bill that would have made it tougher for parents to obtain vaccine exemptions for their children was recently vetoed by the state's governor.

1. What groups of people are more likely to be cynical about vaccinations? Why do you think this is?

CONCLUSION

Scientists and health care agencies continue to educate the public about the basic science behind vaccination, but the controversy over vaccination isn't about the basic science anymore. Anyone can get printed information at the doctor's office or from a health care website using a library computer. The controversy is about two other issues entirely: risk assessment and compliance. "It is a polarizing moment in health care," as Anna Maria Tremonti observed on CBC Radio.

For some people, the issue is moral risk assessment. Parents want to know whether their child is a candidate for medical exemption from vaccination, and except for immuno-compromised children, they're not getting the information. Statistics are not reassuring when a parent can't find out if this child is one of the very few at risk genetically. It's like the philosophical question where a runaway train is speeding toward a loaded commuter train, but could be turned onto a track where it would strike just one person: is it right to risk one person in order to save a train full of people?

For other people, the issue is compliance with perceived fascism, as Louise Habakus writes. The statistics of risks are harder to assess when choice is taken from parents who want to put their children in public schools. Some people believe that when vaccination is imposed by law, citizens have lost the freedom to make informed choices. However, most people still believe that informed choices need to be guided by those who are experts in the field.

Few people want a return to the time when a person had to survive a life-threatening disease to be immune to it. Vaccines to prevent diseases are available, as is information about vaccination, and research continues for improving how vaccination is done. While those who vaccinate themselves and their children constitute the vast majority of Americans and Canadians, a small and vocal percentage continue to speak about the perceived risks of certain vaccines, causing a political discussion that continues to this day.

ABOUT THE EDITOR

Paula Johanson (MA, Canadian Literature) is in the Digital Humanities Graduate Certificate program in the English Department at University of Victoria. Her published nonfiction includes thirty books on science, health, and literature for educational publishers. Born in the early 1960s, she caught measles, mumps, chickenpox, whooping cough (pertussis), rubella, mononucleosis, and influenza, and was vaccinated against smallpox, tetanus, polio, tuberculosis, and influenza. Check out her author website at http://paulajohanson.blogspot.ca!

BIBLIOGRAPHY

"A Parent's Guide to Vaccination." *Healthy Living, Government of Canada*. Updated December 24, 2015. Retrieved March 30, 2016 (http://healthycanadians.gc.ca/publications/healthy-living-vie-saine/parent-guide-vaccination/index-eng.php).

"Addressing Misconceptions on Measles Vaccination." *European Centre for Disease Prevention and Control*. Updated 2016. Retrieved April 8, 2016. (http://ecdc.europa.eu/en/healthtopics/measles/Pages/Addressing-misconceptions-on-measles-vaccination.aspx).

Anderson, Michelle. "5 Facts About Vaccines in the U.S." Pew Research Center, July 17, 2015. (http://www.pewresearch.org/fact-tank/2015/07/17/5-facts-about-vaccines-in-the-u-s/).

Allen, Arthur. *Vaccine: The Controversial History of Medicine's Greatest Lifesaver*, New York, NY: W.W. Norton, 2007.

BC Centre for Disease Control. *I Boost Immunity website. Public Health Association of British Columbia.* Updated 2016. Retrieved April 8, 2016 (http://iboostimmunity.com/node/3).

Belkin, Michael. "Chapter 17: The Vaccine Bubble and the Pharmaceutical Industry." *Vaccine Epidemic* edited by Louise Kuo Habakus and Mary Holland. New York, NY: Skyhorse Publishing, Perseus Book Group, 2011.

Boyd, Lynda. "The Immune System." *Divergent/Convergent Journal of the University 101 Program*. Victoria, BC: University of Victoria University 101 program, 2016.

Bruni, Frank. "California, Camelot and Vaccines." *The New York Times,* July 4, 2015. (http://www.nytimes.com/2015/07/05/opinion/sunday/frank-bruni-california-camelot-and-vaccines.html).

"California Senate Bill No. 277." California State Legislature. (https://leginfo.legislature.ca.gov/faces/billNavClient.xhtml?-bill_id=201520160SB277).

"Council conclusions on vaccinations as an effective tool in public health." *Council of the European Union.* Posted December 1, 2014. Retrieved March 4, 2016 (http://www.consilium.europa.eu/uedocs/cms_data/docs/pressdata/en/lsa/145973.pdf).

Cunningham, Darryl. *How to Fake a Moon Landing: Exposing the Myths of Science Denial.* New York, NY: Abrams ComicArts, 2013.

Doucleff, Michaeleen. "Scientists Crack a 50-year-old Mystery About The Measles Vaccine." *NPR.org* Posted May 17, 2015 (http://www.npr.org/sections/goatsandsoda/2015/05/07/404963436/scientists-crack-a-50-year-old-mystery-about-the-measles-vaccine).

Erickson, Norma. "HPV Vaccine Debate in South Africa." *Sanevax, Inc.*, August 9, 2015. (http://sanevax.org/hpv-vaccine-debate-in-south-africa/).

Erickson, Norma. "Is HPV Vaccine Safety an Illusion Maintained by Suppression of Science?" *Sanevax, Inc.* Posted January 15, 2016. Retrieved February 27, 2016 (http://sanevax.org/hpv-vaccine-safety-an-illusion-maintained-by-suppression-of-science).

Habakus, Louise Kuo, MA. "Every Last One: How to Force Total Vaccine Compliance by Controlling the Conversation and Eliminating Choice." *Wise Traditions in Food, Farming and the Healing Arts,* Vol. 16 # 2, Summer 2015. Washington, DC: Weston A. Price Foundation, 2015, pp. 53-59.

"Jacobson v. Massachusetts." *U.S. Supreme Court.* 197 U.S. 11(1905). Retrieved April 15, 2016. (https://casetext.com/case/henning-jacobson-v-commonwealth-of-massachusetts).

Koerth-Baker, Maggie. "Values and vaccines." *Aeon,* February 16, 2016. (https://aeon.co/essays/anti-vaccination-might-be-rational-but-is-it-reasonable).

Kristof, Nicholas. "The Dangers of Vaccine Denial." *New York Times*. Posted February 8, 2015. Retrieved March 4, 2016 (http://www.nytimes.com/2015/02/08/opinion/sunday/nicholas-kristof-the-dangers-of-vaccine-denial.html).

Leo, Miranda. "Gilbert Doctor's Push for Vaccinations is Personal and Professional." *Cronkite News*, February 10, 2015 (http://cronkitenewsonline.com/2015/02/for-gilbert-doctor-the-push-to-vaccinate-is-personal-as-well-as-professional/).

Loftus, Lauren. "Vaccine Study Aims to Build Common Ground for Parents, Scientific Community." *Cronkite News*, October 2, 2014. (http://cronkitenewsonline.com/2014/10/vaccine-study-aims-to-build-common-ground-for-parents-scientific-community/).

Mannokian, Leslie. "Opinion Piece for the *Idaho Statesman." Wise Traditions in Food, Farming and the Healing Arts.* Vol. 16 # 2, Summer 2015. Washington, DC: Weston A. Price Foundation, 2015, pp. 18-19.

Mnookin, Seth. *The Panic Virus.* New York, NY: Simon & Schuster, 2011.

Nader, Ralph. "Big Pharma—Crony Capitalism Out of Control." *Common Dreams*, November 22, 2014 (http://www.commondreams.org/views/2014/11/22/big-pharma-crony-capitalism-out-control).

"NM v. Hebrew Academy Long Beach Beach et al." *United States District Court Eastern District of New York*. 15-CV-7004(ADS) (AYS) (E.D.N.Y. Jan 09, 2016) Retrieved April 20, 2016 (https://casetext.com/case/nm-ex-rel-lk-v-beach).

Offit, Paul A., M.D. *Deadly Choices: How the Anti-Vaccine Movement Threatens Us All.* New York, NY: Basic Books, Perseus Books Group, 2011.

Pebody, Richard and Kåre Mølbak. "Editorial: Importance of timely monitoring of seasonal influenza vaccine effectiveness." *Eurosurveillance* weekly, Volume 21, Issue 16. Posted April 21, 2016. Retrieved April 22, 2016 (http://www.eurosurveillance.org/ViewArticle.aspx?ArticleId=22454).

"Phillips v. City of New York." *United States Court of Appeals.* January 7, 2015. Retrieved April 10, 2016 (https://casetext.com/case/phillips-ex-rel-bp-v-city-of-ny-2).

Picard, André. "Parents found guilty in son's meningitis death are being rightly punished." *The Globe and Mail.* Posted April 29, 2016. Retrieved April 29, 2016 (http://www.theglobeandmail.com/news/national/parents-found-guilty-in-sons-meningitis-death-are-being-rightly-punished/article29798132).

Raff, Jennifer. "Dear parents, you are being lied to." *Violent Metaphors*. Updated April 19, 2016. Retrieved April 20, 2016 (https://violentmetaphors.com/2014/03/25/parents-you-are-being-lied-to).

Raff, Jennifer. "How to read and understand a scientific paper." *Violent Metaphors*. Updated August 30, 2014. Retrieved July 8, 2016 (https://violentmetaphors.com/2013/08/25/how-to-read-and-understand-a-scientific-paper-2).

Reiss, Dorit Rubinstein. "Italian MMR Autism Decision Overturned." *Skeptical Raptor* blog. Posted April 2, 2016, Retrieved April 12, 2016 (http://www.skepticalraptor.com/skepticalraptorblog.php/italian-mmr-autism-decision-overturned).

Rhodes, John. *The End of Plagues*. New York, NY: St Martin's Press, 2013.

Tremonti, Anna Maria. "Vaccinations: Pro and Anti-Vaxxer Parents Make Their Cases." *The Current, CBC Radio One*. February 9, 2016. (http://www.cbc.ca/radio/thecurrent/vaccinations-pro-and-anti-vaxxer-parents-make-their-cases-1.2952339).

"Understanding How Vaccines Work." *Center for Disease Control, and Immunization Action Coalition*. Updated February 2013. Retrieved March 3, 2016 (http://www.cdc.gov/vaccines/hcp/patient-ed/conversations/downloads/vacsafe-understand-color-office.pdf).

"Vaccine Information for Adults." *CDC-INFO, National Center for Immunization and Respiratory Disease*. Updated January 11, 2016. Retrieved March 4, 2016 (http://www.cdc.gov/vaccines adults/index.html).

CHAPTER NOTES

CHAPTER 1: WHAT THE EXPERTS SAY

"EDITORIAL: IMPORTANCE OF TIMELY MONITORING OF SEASONAL INFLUENZA VACCINE EFFECTIVENESS,"

BY RICHARD PEBODY AND KÅRE MØLBAK

1. Mereckiene J, Cotter S, O'Flanagan D, VENICE III Consortium. National seasonal influenza vaccination survey for 2012-13 influenza season in EU/EEA (provisional data). Available from: http://venice.cineca.org/VENICE_Seasonal_ Influenza_2012-13_v10.pdf
2. Kissling E, Valenciano M, Larrauri A, Oroszi B, Cohen JM, Nunes B, et al. Low and decreasing vaccine effectiveness against influenza A(H3) in 2011/12 among vaccination target groups in Europe: results from the I-MOVE multicentre casecontrol study. Euro Surveill. 2013;18(5):20390.
3. Skowronski DM, Masaro C, Kwindt TL, Mak A, Petric M, Li Y, et al. Estimating vaccine effectiveness against laboratoryconfirmed influenza using a sentinel physician network: www.eurosurveillance.org 3 results from the 2005-2006 season of dual A and B vaccine mismatch in Canada. Vaccine. 2007;25(15):2842-51. Epub 2006 Oct 16.
4. World Health Organization (WHO) Recommended composition of influenza virus vaccines for use in the 2016-2017 northern hemisphere influenza season. Geneva: WHO; Feb 2016. Available from: http://www.who.int/influenza/vaccines/virus/ recommendations/201602_recommendation.pdf?ua=1
5. European Medicines Agency (EMA). Risk-management plans. London: EMA. Available from: http://www.ema.europa.eu/ ema/index.jsp?curl=pages/regulation/document_listing/ document_listing_000360.jsp
6. Leung VK, Cowling BJ, Feng S, Sullivan SG. Concordance of interim and final estimates of influenza vaccine effectiveness: a systematic review. Euro Surveill. 2016;21(16):pii=30202. DOI: 10.2807/1560-7917.ES.2016.21.16.30202
7. Kissling E, Nunes B, Robertson C, Valenciano M, Reuss A,

Larrauri A, et al. I-MOVE multicentre case–control study 2010/11 to 2014/15: Is there within-season waning of influenza type/subtype vaccine effectiveness with increasing time since vaccination? . Euro Surveill. 2016;21(16):pii=30201. DOI: 10.2807/1560-7917.ES.2016.21.16.30201

8. Cuesta JG, Aavitsland P, Englund H, Gudlaugsson Ó, Hauge SH, Lyytikäinen O, et al. Pandemic vaccination strategies and influenza severe outcomes during the influenza A(H1N1) pdm09 pandemic and the post-pandemic influenza season: the Nordic experience. Euro Surveill. 2016;21(16):pii=30208. DOI: 10.2807/1560-7917.ES.2016.21.16.30208
9. Rainwater-Lovett K, Chun K, Lessler J. Influenza outbreak control practices and the effectiveness of interventions in long-term care facilities: a systematic review Influenza Other Respir Viruses. 2014 Jan;8(1):74-82. doi: DOI: 10.1111/irv.12203 . Epub 2013 Nov 7. Review. PMID: 24373292
10. Torner N, Soldevila N, Garcia JJ, Launes C, Godoy P, Castilla J, et al. Effectiveness of non-pharmaceutical measures in preventing pediatric influenza: a case-control study. BMC Public Health. 2015;15:543. DOI: 10.1186/s12889-015-1890-3

CHAPTER 4: WHAT ADVOCACY ORGANIZATIONS SAY

EXCERPT FROM *VACCINE EPIDEMIC: HOW CORPORATE GREED, BIASED SCIENCE, AND COERCIVE GOVERNMENT THREATEN OUR HUMAN RIGHTS, OUR HEALTH, AND OUR CHILDREN*, EDITED BY LOUISE KUO HABAKUS AND MARY HOLLAND

1. http://www.merckmanuals.com/home/brain,-spinal-cord,-and-nerve-disorders/brain-infections/encephalitis
2. http://www.ncbi.nlm.nih.gov/pubmed/21956894
3. Peterson, Melody. *Our Daily Meds: How the Pharmaceutical Companies Transformed Themselves into Slick Marketing Machines*

and Hooked the Nation on Prescription Drugs. New York: Picador, 2009, p.306.
4. https://draxe.com/conventional-medicine-is-the-leading-cause-of-death

"EVERY LAST ONE: HOW TO FORCE TOTAL VACCINE COMPLIANCE BY CONTROLLING THE CONVERSATION AND ELIMINATING CHOICE," BY LOUISE KUO HABAKUS

1. http://www.cdc.gov/mmwr/preview/mmwrhtml/mm6341a1.htm
2. http://www.scribd.com/doc/114630984/Vermont-Vaccine-and-Exemption-Rates-2011-2012-Vaccines-Up-Exemptions-Down
3. http://healthfreedomaction.org/wp-content/uploads/2015/05/HFA-Which-Vax-Kids-Need-5-19-15-3.pdf
4. https://www.cdph.ca.gov/HealthInfo/discond/Documents/Measles_update_4-17-2015_public.pdf
5. http://www.globalresearch.ca/whats-behind-big-pharmas-freak-out-media-blitz-over-measles/5430542
6. http://www.cdc.gov/mmwr/preview/mmwrhtml/mm6341a1.htm
7. http://www.cdc.gov/vaccines/recs/vac-admin/contraindications-vacc.htm
8. http://fearlessparent.org/what-about-the-immunocompromised/
9. http://www.cdc.gov/vaccines/recs/vac-admin/contraindications-misconceptions.htm
10. http://www.nvic.org/Vaccine-Laws/state-vaccine-requirements.aspx
11. http://www.burlingtonfreepress.com/story/news/politics/2015/05/28/shumlin-vaccine-philosophical-exemption/28079499/
12. http://www.foxnews.com/health/2014/04/25/deaths-from-measles-outbreak-may-be-inevitable-as-cases-surge-in-us/
13. http://www.cdc.gov/mmwr/PDF/wk/mm6153.pdf
14. http://jid.oxfordjournals.org/content/189/Supplement_1/S4/F3.expansion.html
15. http://probeinternational.org/library/wp-content/uploads/2014/06/pubhealthreporig00027-0069.pdf
16. http://business.financialpost.com/fp-comment/lawrence-solomon-the-untold-story-of-measles

17. Ibid
18. Source: http://www.reuters.com/article/2011/07/21/us-safety-idUSTRE76K45R20110721
19. http://hva.typepad.com/001_ridbooklet.pdf
20. http://www.chicagomag.com/city-life/March-2014/Why-Is-Vaccine-Refusal-More-Prevalent-Among-the-Affluent/
21. http://portal.unesco.org/en/ev.php-URL_ID=31058&URL_DO=DO_TOPIC&URL_SECTION=201.html
22. http://healthfreedomaction.org/wp-content/uploads/2015/05/ACLU-CA-SB-277-04.02.2015.pdf
23. https://nvicadvocacy.org/members/Home.aspx

CHAPTER 5: WHAT THE MEDIA SAY

"OPINION PIECE FOR THE *IDAHO STATESMAN*, BY LESLIE MANNOKIAN

1. http://www.nytimes.com/2015/02/21/opinion/when-the-government-tells-you-what-to-eat.html?hp&action=click&pgtype=Homepage&module=c-column-top-span-region®ion=c-column-top-span-region&WT.nav=c-column-top-span-region&_r=0
2. http://www.jhsph.edu/research/centers-and-institutes/johns-hopkins-primary-care-policy-center/Publications_PDFs/A154.pdf
3. http://www.forbes.com/sites/erikakelton/2013/07/29/is-big-pharma-addicted-to-fraud/
4. http://www.forbes.com/sites/peterlipson/2015/01/30/anti-vaccine-doctors-should-lose-their-licenses/
5. http://consumer.healthday.com/diseases-and-conditions-information-37/misc-diseases-and-conditions-news-203/parents-still-worried-about-vaccine-safety-636473.html
6. http://www.medpagetoday.com/Pediatrics/GeneralPediatrics/22696
7. http://www.latimes.com/local/education/la-me-school-vaccines-20140903-story.html#page=1
8. http://www.hrsa.gov/vaccinecompensation/authorizinglegislation.pdf
9. http://www.hrsa.gov/vaccinecompensation/statisticsreport.pdf
10. http://www.hrsa.gov/vaccinecompensation/vaccinetable.html
11. http://www.supremecourt.gov/opinions/10pdf/09-152.pdf

12. http://www.nvic.org/injury-compensation/origihanlaw.aspx#
13. http://www.supremecourt.gov/opinions/10pdf/09-152.pdf
14. http://vaers.hhs.gov/index
15. https://autismoevaccini.files.wordpress.com/2012/12/vaccin-dc3a9cc3a8s.pdf
16. http://www.morganverkamp.com/august-27-2014-press-release-statement-of-william-w-thompson-ph-d-regarding-the-2004-article-examining-the-possibility-of-a-relationship-between-mmr-vaccine-and-autism/
17. http://www.huffingtonpost.ca/lawrence-solomon/merck-whistleblowers_b_5881914.html
18. http://www.medicalnewstoday.com/articles/288153.php
19. http://www.academicpedsjnl.net/article/S1876-2859(10)00250-0/abstract
20. http://www.greenmedinfo.com/blog/200-evidence-based-reasons-not-vaccinate-free-research-pdf-download
21. http://healthimpactnews.com/2015/zero-u-s-measles-deaths-in-10-years-but-over-100-measles-vaccine-deaths-reported/
22. http://www.cfr.org/interactives/GH_Vaccine_Map/#map
23. http://gamapserver.who.int/gho/interactive_charts/immunization/mcv/atlas.html
24. http://cid.oxfordjournals.org/content/47/11/1458.full
25. http://healthimpactnews.com/2014/failed-whooping-cough-vaccine-still-being-used-in-the-united-states-outbreaks-blamed-on-unvaccinated/
26. http://articles.mercola.com/sites/articles/archive/2014/06/17/measles-vaccine-failure.aspx
27. http://www.globalresearch.ca/the-disney-measles-outbreak-evidence-reveals-a-failing-measles-vaccine-is-to-blame/5426016
28 http://www.greenmedinfo.com/blog/vaccinated-spreading-measles-who-merck-cdc-documents-confirms
29. http://pediatrics.aappublications.org/content/125/2/e438
30. http://jid.oxfordjournals.org/content/197/Supplement_2/S165.full
31. http://journals.plos.org/plosone/article?id=10.1371/journal.pone.0051653
32. http://www.stjude.org/stjude/v/index.jsp?vgnextoid=20206f9523e70110VgnVCM1000001e0215acRCRD
33.http://www.hopkinsmedicine.org/kimmel_cancer_center/patient_information/Patient%20Guide%20Final.pdf

"DEAR PARENTS, YOU ARE BEING LIED TO," BY JENNIFER RAFF

Links cited throughout the article:
https://www.verywell.com/measles-outbreaks-2633845
http://www.forbes.com/sites/emilywillingham/2014/03/23/worried-about-measles-dont-call-dr-bob-sears/#3f0856665562
https://weather.com/health/news/just-prick-origin-and-evolution-anti-vaccine-movement-20140228?cm_ven=Twitter
http://www.who.int/mediacentre/factsheets/fs286/en/
http://www.cdc.gov/vaccines/vpd-vac/varicella/default.htm
http://www.cdc.gov/flu/index.htm
http://www.cdc.gov/features/pertussis/
http://www.ncbi.nlm.nih.gov/pubmed/10559545
http://www.publichealth.org/public-awareness/understanding-vaccines/vaccine-myths-debunked/
http://pediatrics.aappublications.org/content/123/1/e164.full
http://www.medscape.com/viewarticle/410906_3
http://www.nhs.uk/conditions/vaccinations/pages/benefits-and-risks.aspx
http://cid.oxfordjournals.org/content/48/4/456.full
http://journals.plos.org/plosone/article?id=10.1371/journal.pone.0003140
http://www.jpeds.com/content/JPEDSDeStefano
http://www.ncbi.nlm.nih.gov/pubmed/12949291
http://www.washingtonpost.com/wp-dyn/content/article/2008/09/04/AR2008090401411.html
http://autismsciencefoundation.org/what-is-autism/autism-and-vaccines/
http://www.washingtonpost.com/wp-dyn/content/article/2009/02/12/AR2009021201391.html
http://pediatrics.aappublications.org/content/112/6/1394.full
http://www.sciencedirect.com/science/article/pii/0048969795047024
https://violentmetaphors.com/2013/11/22/why-anti-vaxers-hate-the-nvicp-and-just-what-is-it-anyway-by-colin-mcroberts/
https://pediatricinsider.wordpress.com/2013/01/22/dr-bobs-alternative-vaccine-schedule-he-made-it-up/
http://www.vaccines.gov/basics/protection/
http://autismsciencefoundation.org/what-is-autism/beware-of-non-evidence-based-treatments/

http://www.cdc.gov/mmwr/preview/mmwrhtml/mm6019a5.htm
https://violentmetaphors.com/2013/08/14/the-truth-about-vaccinations-your-physician-knows-more-than-the-university-of-google/comment-page-5/#comment-1797
http://www.bmj.com/content/342/bmj.c5347
https://www.sciencebasedmedicine.org/cashing-in-on-fear-the-danger-of-dr-sears/
http://thinkingmomsrevolution.com/an-open-letter-to-my-facebook-friends/
http://www.cc.com/video-clips/gh6urb/the-colbert-report-neil-degrasse-tyson-pt--1
http://www.jennymccarthybodycount.com/PreventableIllnesses.html
http://www.salon.com/2014/03/20/measles_outbreak_vaccine_trutherism_now_officially_a_public_health_crisis/
http://theweek.com/articles/450101/worrying-rise-antivaccination-movement#comment-1272032755
http://www.nytimes.com/2005/11/08/us/5-cases-of-polio-in-amish-group-raise-new-fears.html?_r=0
https://www.aap.org/en-us/advocacy-and-policy/aap-health-initiatives/immunization
http://www.ncbi.nlm.nih.gov/pubmedhealth/PMH0072548/
http://www.historyofvaccines.org/content/articles/vaccine-development-testing-and-regulation
https://www.healthychildren.org/English/safety-prevention/immunizations/pages/How-do-Vaccines-Work.aspx
http://rationalwiki.org/wiki/Andrew_Wakefield
http://www.bmj.com/content/342/bmj.c5347
https://en.wikipedia.org/wiki/Andrew_Wakefield
http://cid.oxfordjournals.org/content/48/4/456.full
http://genetics.thetech.org/original_news/news49
http://www.ncbi.nlm.nih.gov/pubmed/19805709
http://autismsciencefoundation.org/
http://www.mlanet.org/resources/userguide.html
https://violentmetaphors.com/2013/08/25/how-to-read-and-understand-a-scientific-paper-2/

GLOSSARY

autism A neurological condition present from early childhood, in which a person has difficulty in communicating and forming relationships with other people and in using language and abstract concepts.

childhood diseases Diseases caused by microbes such as viruses or bacteria that spread from person to person, which can be common in childhood and may be life-threatening.

conscience Self-awareness; in this context, the ability to choose whether or not to consent to orders from a government authority, based on one's religion and moral beliefs.

fascism An authoritarian and nationalist system of government and social controls, forcibly suppressing any criticism or opposition.

herd immunity If nearly all the members of a herd of animals or large group of people are immune to a disease, when the disease is introduced to the group it does not spread among them to the few who are not immune.

immune system The body's interconnecting system through blood and lymph systems, for recognizing and resisting challenges to the body's health from other organisms, usually microbes that enter the body.

immunity The ability for the body to recognize and resist a viral or bacterial disease without becoming ill.

immunization The process of making people immune to a disease, usually by vaccinating them.

influenza Also called more generally "the flu," this viral infection causes fever and aches and is highly contagious.

jargon Special words and phrases used by a group or profession, that can be hard to understand without context

Luddite A person who fears and hates technology; named for Ned Ludd and activist textile workers in the 1800s who destroyed new textile machinery used to get around standard quality and labor practices, calling for machines that made good fabric operated by trained journeymen earning a living wage.

mercury A heavy metal, which is liquid at room temperature; used in some medicine and antibiotics to treat some infectious diseases, although it has been largely replaced with newer medications.

serological Having to do with the science that deals with serum and other bodily fluids, especially blood serum.

thimerosol A medical preservative containing a form of mercury which in the past was added to the diphtheria/pertussis/tetanus vaccine.

vaccination The process of introducing a vaccine into people to make them immune to a disease, usually by injection.

vaccine A substance made from a virus or bacteria, usually in weakened or killed form, which can be used to expose people to a disease so they develop immunity without causing them to become ill.

FOR MORE INFORMATION

BOOKS

Cunningham, Darryl. *How to Fake a Moon Landing: Exposing the Myths of Science Denial.* New York, NY: Abrams ComicArts, 2013.

Friedman, Stacy. *The Anti-Vaccination Movement.* Santa Barbara, CA: Greenwood, 2016.

Miller, Neil Z. *Miller's Review of Critical Vaccine Studies: 400 Important Scientific Papers Summarized for Parents and Researchers.* Santa Fe, NM: New Atlantean Press, 2016.

Offit, Paul A., M.D. *Deadly Choices: How the Anti-Vaccine Movement Threatens Us All.* New York, NY: Basic Books, Perseus Books Group, 2011.

Rhodes, John. *The End of Plagues.* New York, NY: St Martin's Press, 2013.

Rosner, Lisa. *Vaccination and Its Critics: A Documentary and Reference Guide.* Santa Barbara, CA: Greenwood, 2016.

WEBSITES

The History of Vaccines
www.historyofvaccines.org
Created by The College of Physicians of Philadelphia, one of the oldest medical societies in the United States, this award-winning education website features not only a history of vaccines, but activities, articles, and answers to most frequently asked questions about vaccinations.

Immunization Action Coalition
www.vaccineinformation.org
The Immunization Action Coalition is one of the leading advocates for vaccinations and their website is a resource for people of all ages about vaccination and vaccine-preventable diseases.

Public Health Association of British Columbia: I Boost Immunity
iboostimmunity.com
Sponsored by the Public Health Association of British Columbia, *I Boost Immunity* features quizzes about vaccines; for every question answered correctly, one vaccine will be donated to someone in need.

INDEX